Finding Gilbert

A Promise Fulfilled

Finding Gilbert
A Promise Fulfilled

Marshall & McClintic Publishing
200 Coyote Street #1122, Nevada City, CA 95959
MarshallMcClinticPublishing.com

This book is set in Times New Roman Text.
Printed in the United States of America
First Edition: June 2018
First Edition ISBN-13: 978-0-9910446-7-2

Cover Photos
Front and Back Covers: US Navy Ships, Normandy Invasion, June 1944
Front Cover:
Bottom Left: Gilbert DesClos held by an American Soldier, June 1944
Center: Donald Kenneth Johnson, official Navy photo, 1944
Bottom Right: Sharon Johnson, age 5 and Diane Johnson, author, age 3 with father Donald, as he left for the Korean War, Fall 1951
Author photo: Carrie Dobbs 2018

To my father,
who taught me that love
is the most important thing

and to my husband, Landon,
for being the love of my life

Reviews for Finding Gilbert:

Writer's Digest Self-Published Book Awards
Judge's commentary:
Finding Gilbert is not only a memoir, it is a mystery. It is also a multi-layered story: through looking for Gilbert, the author also finds, in many ways, herself and her family.

The story is told well, in the author's straightforward and honest voice, and the reader feels a part of her journey. And it's satisfying that the book doesn't end when Gilbert is found; that happens just a little more than halfway through the story. The story continues with her life and Gilbert's and his family's life.

The book has poignant moments; for instance, when Gilbert tells her that his father promised to come back for him. The author does a nice job of not layering these with a lot of sentiment, but letting the story speak for itself. She also weaves in background information, including family history and world history, without bogging (the reader) down in unneeded exposition.

Her choice to use narrative form is a good one; the story is believable and she makes dialogue and events that she obviously was not there for work.

Writer's Digest E-book Awards
Judge's commentary:
Finding Gilbert is a testament to how even the most seemingly unrelated happenings can have long-term consequences. During the 1944 invasion of Normandy, the author's father, Donald Kenneth Johnson, took Gilbert, a seven-year-old French orphan under his wing.

Although he attempted to adopt the boy, the capriciousness of fate tore them apart and Gilbert remained in France while Johnson went back to his home in California.

Author Diane Covington-Carter grew up on her Dad's stories of Gilbert, feeling as though he was the brother she'd never had a chance to know. She made a pilgrimage to Normandy in the early 1990s, a few years after her father's death, setting into motion a far-reaching sequence of events that impacted several generations.

Part memoir, part detective story, this book is a testament to both persistence and the enduring power of love. The author faithfully recounts misunderstandings, bumps in the road and rewards as the two families' fates begin to intertwine and they populate each other's lives. This makes for compelling reading.

The power of a book whose underlying theme is at the end, 'it's all about who you love and letting them know' is undeniable.

Readers' praise for Finding Gilbert:

This book is truly, one of the top books I have ever read. I am grateful that Diane was able to develop her love for writing so we all can delight in the treasure of her writing style and stories. It was extremely hard to lay aside her words to carry on with my daily tasks.

Started it last night, made myself eventually go to bed; woke up at 3 a.m., read till 5 a.m. and finished it when I woke again at 6:30! Wonderful book. Obviously I loved it!

I just finished reading Finding Gilbert. It was really a great story. I couldn't put the book down. Your book was more than I expected. Thank you for writing it.

I started reading the book the afternoon I received it and kept reading into the evening until I finished. A friend had recommended the book to me because my father had served in WWII and always spoke of his time in France with respect.

Even though this book is a memoir, it reads like a novel. There are enough twists and turns to keep you reading and the story is easily accessible to any post war or current family member. The search for Gilbert is a major focus, but the richness and delight in other themes that are revealed as surprises of destiny are moving, provoking and lasting.

This book would appeal to anyone interested in embracing the destinies of life's paths, and the synchronicity of events making sense in the span of a lifetime. I also learned more about the Americans who served in WWII and my compassion for their service and bravery has deepened. I appreciate this author for sharing herself and her loved ones with us. I am left with an experience of celebration and love.

If anyone reading this knows Steven Spielberg or Tom Hanks, please send this book to them immediately. Finding Gilbert will make a remarkable movie. This story has everything a great movie would want—family, Normandy, a young woman's story of growing up after WW1I. You will love reading Diane's story.

This book is beautifully crafted, an exceptional story about honoring the past and the connections that link us. A profound time in our history is woven in with the story of a loving, tender woman as she emerges into her own destiny, healing and full power. My compassion and ability to listen to the nuances grew as I read this story. I loved it!

Wonderful heartfelt account of a daughter's love for her father's memory. The story flows through both historic and personal times taking you from the yellow Formica kitchen table of the 50's to the French countryside of WWII. Diane's gifted writing lets you experience this lifetime search, bridging two generations, following the heart. Bravo!

I loved this book, very easy to read, well written and clearly a lot of research went into it. A very emotional read that left me thinking that it will make a wonderful movie. A touching story of a father's war experience and its impact on his daughter and those he knew in France.

Even though I had read the book she wrote after this one I enjoyed her every word. I laughed and cried! Her writing evokes so many emotions. Diane is a great writer and I will enjoy more of her works.

This is the second book by Diane Covington-Carter I have read. I can't add much more than others before me except to say how much it moved me. I heartily and sincerely recommend it.

Finding Gilbert is a beautiful story about Diane Covington-Carter miraculously finding her orphan "brother" after 50 years. This book has everything; history, adventure, wisdom, quests, stories, love. Bravissimo Diane! Looking forward to the next chapter and another great memoir.

What an amazing, surprising, touching work this book is. Diane's and her father's story (which really reads more like a can't-put-down-novel) is moving and touching beyond compare. Not only is the story fascinating, but it is told expertly. Diane is a true storyteller, both as a guide and a crafts woman. Thank you for sharing this story, all of it, with the world. I will cherish my signed copy of the book for all of my days.

I loved this book! It's my favorite of Diane's 3 memoirs. She brought me to tears many times. I couldn't put it down. It was amazing that she was able to find Gilbert and give him the closure he needed, to let him know that her dad never forgot him. Then that Gilbert's family became her second family was so touching. I read this book, because I had recently been to Normandy. I could visualize her father there with this young boy. It made such an impression on me. This is a must read for WWII buffs.

A memoir filled with touching poignancy, and much tenderness. The author weaves a wonderful story filled with personal struggle and rich rewards. The success she finds in searching for an orphan boy in France from World War II and the strong bond with her father, form the nucleus of the story. Without relying on gimmicks or over sentimentality, Diane Covington-Carter displays an adept touch in telling a truly heartfelt story.

I read Finding Gilbert on a recent flight to California. What a beautiful, touching story! I resonated with much of it. Many beautiful moments moved me and the book has stayed with me. Diane Covington-Carter writes at such depth and her story affected me deeply.

What a story! This is a story of the endurance of love and the impact one can have on generations. The story relates to many things we all encounter in life: joy, hope, kindness, love, regret and how they all last, when truly experienced, for a lifetime. I very much enjoyed the connection of Diane's father with Gilbert but even more so in her own life. Her daddy strove to make others around him feel LOVED. Through the kindness of a meal or an encouraging word to his child as an adult, he was a highlight of the story for me. It is a very well written story and I am so glad to have had the chance to read it.

I've read this book twice and was so touched by the story and the devotion of her dad to this young boy Gilbert and to Diane, and how that bought the two together after her father's death. I highly recommend this book to anyone and everyone. You will not soon forget this story of love.

Finding Gilbert is a compelling story of relationships formed in the midst of the trauma of war, life resuming more normal patterns, and then the joy of relationships renewed. One man's reaching out to a child created a ripple of connection through his wider family, to eventually reach across the seas once again and unite a group of people in a heart-warming way. Good job Ms. Covington-Carter.

This was a powerful memoir. I couldn't put it down. It really absorbed me. It is a great reminder of how far an act of kindness can stretch–through generations.

What a great read. I don't cry often, but this story is something special. I'm going to buy printed copies for my Francophile family!

I adored this book! I cried with absolute joy! Reading Diane's story has become one of the highlights of my life. What an honor to her dad and of course a gift for Gilbert. It's as if her story is now a small part of my life, in that I can rejoice with her.

I discovered a tale that made me laugh and cry at the same time. It continued on to leave me with a warm feeling about love and the human condition.

This is a wonderfully written story that warmed my heart.

A well-crafted memoir. I enjoyed the weaving of her father's past and the part he played in Normandy in WWII with the author's childhood and unfoldment and then with the life of Gilbert. Covington-Carter demonstrates the interconnection of our lives and the importance of one human caring for another.

Table of Contents

They seem very ordinary
those moments that change
our lives forever

In reality, the moments just
before them were ordinary
and then everything stopped
or glowed or vibrated
and stood out
from the moment before

And looking back
it is clear
how life changed forever
in that instant

Prologue

Sunlight sparkled on the water of the English Channel, seagulls circled and dove and the rhythmic sound of the waves breaking in the distance floated up to where I stood at the top of the cliff.

With seven other American tourists, I had spent the day learning about the Normandy Invasion. Our French tour guide, Marcel, had shown us beaches with the code names of Sword, Juno, Gold, Utah—and now Omaha.

"See that beach down there?" Marcel pointed to the long expanse of sand below us that stretched out to sea.

"Peaceful, right?" We all nodded.

"Well, on June 6, 1944, that beach was anything but peaceful. You're looking down at the American landing beach that became known as "Bloody Omaha," for all the American soldiers who lost their lives there in the early hours of D-Day."

A seagull called. Waves sighed. Marcel turned to gesture at the fields behind us. "The cemetery behind you was designated as a piece of American soil in honor of the soldiers who were never able to return home."

We turned to look at the manicured green space, where almost ten thousand white crosses lined up in perfect symmetrical rows as far as we could see. Visitors whispered as they walked among the crosses, some searching for the name of a loved one. A baby's cry broke the stillness.

"Did you say that your father was in the D-Day invasion?" Marcel gestured to me.

"Yes, he was," I said. "In fact, he was one of those who landed on Omaha Beach. Now I know how lucky I was that he came back so that I could be born."

Marcel shook his head in agreement.

I'd never been interested in history. In school, I doodled and daydreamed during class, memorized dates for a test, then promptly forgot them. I didn't see how what had happened in a bunch of wars in the past mattered in my life.

But two years before, my father had passed away. All my life, he'd told stories of his time in France during the war, and losing him made those memories more precious. I realized that I had a personal relationship to this historic event and with the 50th anniversary of the D-Day invasion coming up the following June 1994, found myself genuinely interested.

I'd begun to realize that my father's stories had influenced my life in ways that I was still discovering. And so I'd journeyed to France to learn all that I could. I was going to write a story that would come out on the 50th anniversary of D-Day, describing Dad's stories and their impact on my life.

The day had been moving and powerful. We visited small museums full of photos and memorabilia, uniforms and newspaper clippings. We watched footage of old newsreels, with Eisenhower speaking to shiny faced young men who were excited and eager to go into battle.

We learned that over five thousand ships, eleven thousand planes, eighteen thousand paratroopers and two hundred thousand soldiers had descended on the five landing beaches in the early hours of June 6th, 1944. The cost was high; more than 9,000 allied troops had been killed or wounded. We studied a giant relief map depicting the planes and ships, trying to understand the enormity of it all.

Our final stop of the day was the American Cemetery in Colleville-sur-Mer, situated on the cliff above Omaha Beach. Our guide gave us some time to walk around the impeccably manicured one hundred and seventy-two acres. As I tried to digest all I'd seen and heard, I was grateful for the time alone.

I wandered into the small chapel on the grounds. On the ceiling, an artist had rendered an angel watching over a soldier and the inscription on the wall read, "Think not only upon their passing, remember the glory of their spirit."

I reflected on those words as I walked back to the cliffs again and sat down on a bench to try to sort out all my thoughts. Remembering my dad, the tears began to fall. I turned my face into the chilly fall wind off the sea and breathed in the fresh, salty air.

Dad's stories of the war had seemed like just that— stories, not completely real. But now I knew that he'd been a part of the largest land and sea invasion in the history of the world. That made me wonder: after living so close to life-and-death, how had Dad and the other soldiers returned to a normal life? Nothing else would be as real as that ever again. So they must have been caught—between wanting to forget and not being able to.

No wonder there'd been a post-war baby boom, of which I was a part. After so much death and destruction,

3

family life and babies must have seemed like a balm, a blessing.

I adored my father and thought I knew him well. But there was so much here he'd seen and experienced that he hadn't talked about. Why hadn't I encouraged him to come back to France again? Why hadn't I asked more questions and paid more attention, before it was too late?

As I looked out over the water, I remembered Dad's stories about the seven-year-old French orphan, Gilbert, who Dad had befriended during his five months in Normandy. Dad even tried to adopt the boy and bring him home.

In the months before my father died, when he talked about Gilbert, he'd seemed wistful. "I wonder what ever happened to him," he said.

Now, as I stood where Dad and Gilbert had become so close, I thought again about the little boy who could have become my older brother. Just as Dad's stories about the war gained substance from my being there, Gilbert, too, became more real. He was no longer just a character in one of Dad's stories.

Where would Gilbert be now? I wasn't even sure how to spell his last name. I just knew how it sounded—DesClos, DuClos? After fifty years, what chance would there be of tracking him down? And if I did somehow find him, would he even remember Dad? It all seemed impossible.

But maybe because I was where it had all happened, the idea began to haunt me.

What if Gilbert was still out there somewhere, remembering my dad?

What if I could find him?

Part I

1944

1

JUNE 1944

Plymouth, England

My father, Donald Kenneth Johnson, a lieutenant junior grade in the 111th Battalion of the Seabees, the Civil Engineering Corps of the U.S. Naval Reserves, held a clipboard and looked out over the English Channel towards France.

A crisp wind off the water blew sand sideways and the sky threatened rain. He had just dismissed his men and took a moment to survey the scene in front of him. They had completed their project of building the Rhino Ferries, the flat-bottomed pontoon barges to be used in the upcoming invasion. Many bobbed and swayed in the water in front of him.

The Rhino Ferries, powered by two 143-horse power Chrysler outboard marine motors, measured one hundred seventy-five feet long and could hold forty vehicles and up to six hundred tons, their strength equal to a civilian highway bridge. During the invasion, soldiers, trucks and tanks would be able to unload from the ships onto the ferries and cram into every available inch for the trip to the landing beaches.

One of the Seabees' mottos, "Can Do!" was perfect for my father, who was tall and strong and enjoyed getting things done. His Scandinavian heritage and his childhood growing up on a farm had taught him the meaning and value of hard work. He enjoyed being an engineer, using his mind to design and create real and practical things in the world, bridges, roads, water systems and in this case, ferries. His light blue eyes reflected his kind nature. At twenty-nine, he was considered "old" to the young sailors of eighteen, but they looked up to him and valued his engineering knowledge. He and his crew had been working long hours for months to prepare for the invasion.

Everyone was anxious now to get going; the waiting had put the men on edge and decreased morale. Evenings they gathered in the neighborhood pub to drink warm beer, even learning some of the local songs. Dad whistled one of the tunes as he walked back to the barracks, "I've got sixpence, jolly, jolly sixpence, I've got sixpence, to last me all my life…"

He was proud of the work he and his men had done to build the ferries. Eisenhower had just given the word for the invasion. They were ready.

JUNE 6TH, 1944

The stormy weather made the trip across the English Channel cold, wet and rough. But this was it. My father and his men felt the excitement and importance of being a part of the Allied invasion of France. No one slept that night as the boats crossed the choppy channel; they drank strong, hot coffee to stay awake. Dad and his crews had been assigned to land at Omaha Beach; the other Americans would land on Utah Beach, further west.

The bad weather created more problems than just rough seas. The early morning air strikes missed their targets above

Omaha Beach, due to thick storm clouds. But no one knew that until it was too late.

Just before dawn, when the first landing craft arrived on Omaha and soldiers spilled out, the Germans opened fire. The strong seas sank twenty-seven out of the twenty-nine tanks that were supposed to help; the soldiers who were not dead or wounded had no cover from the German fire on the flat beach.

The second wave of reinforcements encountered the same withering gunfire. In addition, the high waves and strong currents took the landing craft off course; soldiers were not able to land at their assigned sectors, creating even more chaos.

After hours of this disastrous scenario, a Naval destroyer pulled in close and blasted the cliffs, blowing up some of the German bunkers. In addition, by late morning, a few brave soldiers scaled the hill to take out the Germans behind the guns. By nightfall, after a day of brutal fighting, the beach was relatively secured.

The next morning, when my father and his men made the trip to the shore, rows of bodies lay on the beach, waiting to be identified as the tide rushed in and sea gulls swarmed, screamed and dove.

There were no words for that horrific scene. Dad, an officer, felt like an older brother to the young sailors of eighteen who were under his command. Some of them were vomiting, others crying as he struggled to keep his own composure. "War was hell," the saying went, and this scene was about as close to hell as he could imagine.

He thanked God and fate that he and his men had not been assigned to land the previous day and said a prayer for those young men lying there who had lost their lives and their futures the day before.

He had worked with his men for months in England and knew that if they could focus on the projects ahead, it could take their mind off this nightmarish scene. Their Rhino Ferries, called by some a "secret weapon," had been a huge success in getting troops and heavy equipment from ship to shore on D-Day at a speed both unprecedented and unanticipated by the Germans.

One of the Seabees' mottos was, *"Construimus, batuimus,"* "We Build, We Fight" and their mascot, a feisty-looking bee, carried a drill in one hand and a gun in the other. The Seabees had their work cut out for them again. They had to transform the beach and the cliffs beyond into a major staging area for the next crucial phase of the war. Three million troops would land there in the coming months. The success of the war depended on it.

There were the roads to carve out from the beach up to the campsite on the hill and beyond, the camp and the airstrip to build. The soldiers needed hot showers, the cooks needed mess tents to prepare meals and the doctors needed the infirmary set up and supplied.

In addition, there was the continuous job of unloading the huge supply ships daily, crammed with the material of war—the gasoline, tanks, Jeeps, guns, ammunition and medical supplies, not to mention the thousands of tons of food needed to feed the men.

German planes strafed the beach, snipers' shots rang out and there was the constant danger of stepping onto one of the thousands of land mines hidden everywhere in the rough, grassy earth or on the beach. Dad carried a standard military issue 38-caliber pistol on his belt. He had earned a medal for sharpshooting, but his job was to build first, then to fight.

He and his men had a job to do and they would do it, "on the double."

2

Seven-year-old Gilbert DesClos sat in the tall grass on the cliff above Omaha Beach and shivered in the sea air. The sun rose over the trees as he hugged his bony knees tight to his chest and pulled his worn, wool sweater around him. Ever since the arrival of *les Américains* weeks before, his world had changed. Overnight, a military camp had materialized on the empty field just below his home in Normandy. For Gilbert, an orphan, it was a boy's dream. His caretaker, Madame Bisson, had to drag him in at night.

Now he watched, wide-eyed, as Jeeps roared up the road and men in white caps scurried about, emptying trucks loaded with guns, ammunition, food, and giant duffel bags. He yawned as the smell of bacon, eggs, coffee, and toast wafted up from a massive tent. As he tilted his small head back, breathing in the aromas, his stomach growled.

My father held a clipboard and checked off the morning's accomplishments. The infirmary tent was complete; now the medics and doctors had a decent place to treat soldiers. The showers worked and the hot water had raised morale.

He and his men had been busy since dawn; it was now noon. He dismissed them, then took a moment and touched the breast pocket that held the photo of my mother and their two young sons. It had been so long since he'd seen them and he hadn't received a letter in weeks.

When he turned to go, he spied something moving in the tall grass on the hill. He tensed and his hand moved instinctively to the gun on his belt. But he paused, knowing they had secured this area, and peered into the grass. He thought he saw a head. Was that a child?

He lifted his hand in a wave. A small hand waved back. It *was* a child. Dad paused, then beckoned. There was a moment of hesitation, and then a boy, barely taller than the grass, made his way down. Dad knelt to look into the child's thin face.

The little guy looked about five years old; his worn, brown sweater had holes and barely covered his bony torso. His legs stuck out like sticks from his baggy, tan shorts. Dad wondered where he had come from and thought he looked like he could use a good meal. At least they had plenty of food—in fact, they threw out a lot each day, and he was determined to do something about that when his turn came to oversee the mess tent.

The boy's clear blue eyes twinkled as he smiled, then looked down. Dad searched his brain for the French that he'd been reviewing. He'd thrown his high-school French book into his wooden sea locker when he found out he was going overseas and had studied it on the ship and some evenings since the landings, when he wasn't too tired.

Dad knelt down and tried out some of his words with Gilbert.

"Comment vous appelez-vous?" No, he corrected himself—this was a child and you used the familiar form of *"tu."* *"Comment t'appelles-tu?"* he asked. What is your name?

"Gilbert," pronounced "Jeelbeert," came the soft answer, barely audible.

"Moi, je m'appelle Donald, Donald Johnson."

Gilbert smiled as Dad shook his hand.

"As-tu faim?" Are you hungry?

The smell of roast beef, carrots and potatoes, apple pie and coffee drifted out of the mess tent and mixed with the fresh sea air. Other officers rushed past into the tent and Dad felt his own hunger pangs. He'd eaten breakfast at 0600 hours. Church bells in the nearby village rang out the noon hour.

"Veux-tu déjeuner avec moi?" Do you want to have lunch with me? Dad asked Gilbert.

Gilbert nodded his head, so Dad took his small hand and led him into the officers' mess tent. Once inside, he picked the boy up and jiggled him a little, like he always did with his sons at home. Gilbert giggled and hung on, then his eyes became wide as he took in all the food spread out in front of them. Dad took a tray and filled a plate for himself and one for Gilbert.

During lunch, Gilbert kept his head down, eating his food with relish, but from time to time, peeked up and smiled. It looked to Dad as though the child hadn't eaten that well in years, if ever.

Dad talked to the other officers, discussing the plans for the afternoon: who would oversee the unloading of the ships, which group was going to continue on the project of camp construction and distribution of the newly arrived sea bags and mail for the enlisted men.

But he kept looking over at Gilbert, who sat close by. As he watched the boy eat, he patted him on the head and smiled at him. *"Très bien,"* he told him. Very good. Gilbert smiled back.

13

When it was time to get back to work, Dad led Gilbert outside, knelt down again and tried to remember what else he could say in French. He managed to say that he had to work, but invited Gilbert to return that evening at dinnertime, 1800 hours, six o'clock.

Dad got into his Jeep to head down to the beach and paused to look back. Gilbert stood in the same spot, watching. A soldier walked by and saluted Dad. Gilbert raised his hand in a salute, giggled and then ran up the path and out of sight.

My father sighed. The little guy was so cute and he had gobbled up his lunch. Then the work of the afternoon ahead pulled him back and he sped off to oversee the unloading of the ships that had pulled in with the high tide.

With a difference of over forty feet between the low and high tides, they brought the huge ships in at high water. Then at low water, with the ships high and dry, they could open up the front end and unload directly onto the beach. Each day, the Seabees unloaded hundreds of thousands of tons of war material.

They had to stay alert, though. The tide rushed back in at a speed "faster than a galloping horse" and once it reached the ship, they couldn't move fast enough to close the ship's hull back up and to get everything to high ground. They had lost tanks, Jeeps and supplies under the water a few weeks before when Dad left someone else in charge; he wanted to make sure that it didn't happen again.

At 1800 hours, Dad walked toward the officers' mess tent. He'd showered, the warmth of the water relaxing his tired muscles, and had changed into a clean uniform.

Gilbert stood where they'd said goodbye earlier. The same old sweater and shorts, the same shy smile. Dad took his hand, then hoisted him up and headed into dinner.

14

The menu was fried chicken, mashed potatoes, corn, biscuits with butter and chocolate cake. Gilbert didn't eat as much as he had at lunch; it was clear that he wasn't used to so much food. But he sat close to Dad and smiled his shy smile, taking big breaths between bites, as if willing himself to eat as much as he could.

After dinner, Dad knelt close to Gilbert. "*Bonsoir,*" he said. "*À demain.*" Goodnight. Until tomorrow.

He watched the boy scamper up the path and out of sight.

As the days and weeks of the summer of 1944 passed, Gilbert blossomed, his skinny body filled out and his cheeks became plump and rosy with the summer sun. The comfort of the hot meals in the officers' mess tent, seated next to Dad, assuaged his physical hunger, but the time and attention Dad gave him strengthened him in other ways. He lost some of his shyness. He smiled, laughed out loud sometimes and giggled often, especially when Dad carried him around on his shoulders.

Gilbert soon began riding along in the Jeep down to the beach, when Dad supervised the unloading of ships. When my father oversaw construction projects in the camp, Gilbert tagged along. If Dad left camp with his crew to rebuild a road or a blown-out bridge, the boy waited at the gate for his return.

My father's French improved, and Gilbert learned to say "hello," "goodbye," "thank you," "Jeep," "ship," and "ice cream." He could also say, "Lieutenant Donald Johnson."

The other officers and soldiers enjoyed including Gilbert in the life of the camp. In fact, the boy seemed to help ease their homesickness. But Gilbert's favorite was Dad. Dad began to piece together that Gilbert lived nearby in a house

15

with another child, Georgette, and her grandmother, Madame Bisson. He was an orphan, with no parents and no family.

Dad had known that war would be brutal and it had been. He'd lived nightmares that would haunt him for the rest of his life. But in the midst of all that horror, there had been this gift, this little boy, who had become a part of his daily life. He found himself wondering about Gilbert's future. He began to wish he could somehow take him home to America.

Late one September afternoon, Dad drove his Jeep into the nearby city of Caen where he had heard there were some government offices. Winding through the bombed-out streets filled with rubble, he found the tiny office. With a French dictionary in hand and some sentences he had written out the night before, like French homework, he asked the man behind the desk if he could apply to adopt a French orphan and bring him back to America.

Even with his limited French, he understood the response.

"Non, ce n'est pas possible." No, it isn't possible.

He'd argued, trying to understand the more extended explanation, but just couldn't follow what the official was saying.

Defeated, he steered the Jeep back to the camp, his shoulders slumped from the disappointment. He'd grown to love Gilbert and knew that the boy had grown to love him. He had hoped Gilbert could just be added in to his family.

My mother hadn't been thrilled, writing that Dad should come home and get to know the two young sons he already had. But he pleaded with her in his letters and over the months, she gave in, since he felt that strongly.

It all had seemed possible. Now he had just been told that it wouldn't be. But surely, there must be a way.

Dad knew that when his orders changed, saying goodbye to Gilbert would be painful. He was determined that the time he had left in France be as rich as possible with the boy.

On the long evenings, some of the officers organized football or softball games. Dad had played some softball in college and was a good, strong hitter. Gilbert sat on the sidelines and watched, clapping and smiling when Dad hit the ball with a thwack and ran around the bases.

One night, Dad decided Gilbert should have a chance to play. He led him to home plate, stood behind him and together they held the bat. When the ball hit the bat, Dad swooped Gilbert up and they raced around the bases. All the men played in slow motion, making sure that the pair made it into home plate. Gilbert beamed with excitement when everyone cheered at their success.

In early October, as the days began to shorten and the wind off the sea became cold, Dad and his crew drove to Bayeux to repair a bridge. In the quaint village, many of the shops remained intact. Among them, Dad saw what looked like a children's shop, *Petit Bateau*, the Little Boat.

Once the work of the morning flowed smoothly, he put a junior officer in charge and walked over to the shop. The bell on the door tinkled a cheery greeting as he opened it and went in. The lights had not yet been restored to the building and it was dark inside, except for the dim light of a gas lamp. But the elderly woman in the back smiled and came forward with a cheery *"Bonjour."* He smiled back and tried to explain what he was looking for.

"Pour un garçon." For a boy. He held up his hand for Gilbert's height and gestured to establish the boy's slight frame. Dad pointed to his own shirt, pants, and to a sweater he saw nearby. The woman bustled about, opening drawers and ruffling through shelves, then walked over to the dusty

window to show him some tan shorts, a light blue shirt and a dark blue sweater.

"*Très bien,*" Very good, Dad exclaimed and pointed to a package of clean white underwear.

"*Et les souliers?*" And shoes?

When Dad nodded, she asked, "*Quelle taille?*" What size?

Dad paused, then estimated Gilbert's shoe size with his hands. The woman searched through the shoeboxes that were lined up along a sidewall, mumbling to herself in French, then brought out a pair of brown leather shoes that looked to be just about right. And a pair of brown socks to match.

"*Et un chapeau?*" And a hat?

"*Mais oui!*" Dad replied.

She produced a wool beret, dark blue to match the sweater. At the last instant, he grabbed a small stuffed bear that was propped up on a display.

As Dad got the Francs out of his wallet and paid for the clothes, the proprietress wrapped them up in brown paper and tied the parcel with string. He whistled as he left the shop, calling out "*Merci, au revoir,*" to the owner. She returned the greeting and waved.

Back at the camp, Gilbert waited, smiling and waving when Dad pulled in. As soon as Dad was free, he grabbed Gilbert and swung him up onto his shoulders. He told the boy that he had a big surprise for him, but first there was something they had to do. Dad walked over to the showers tent and explained to Gilbert that he wanted him to take a shower.

"*Non!*" Gilbert exclaimed in horror and fear, trying to run away. He had never been inside the shower tent or taken a shower and howled like a frightened, trapped animal.

Dad knelt down, took Gilbert's shoulders and looked into the boy's eyes.

"*Gilbert, Gilbert, calme-toi.*"

Dad explained that after the shower, Gilbert would get his big surprise, in the brown packet, tied up with the string. Gilbert sniffed and hiccupped, his small mouth puckered into a pout, but he let Dad take off his worn clothes and coax him to step under the warm water. Dad motioned for him to use the soap, to wash his face, and behind his ears, then his hair, then wrapped him up in a towel to dry.

When Dad opened the brown parcel and showed the clean little boy the new clothes, Gilbert gaped.

"*Pour toi,*" Dad said. For you.

Gilbert stared, his mouth open, then began to shiver, still staring, unmoving.

"*Allez.*" Let's go. Dad helped Gilbert to put on the clean, new underwear, then the shorts, the shirt and the sweater, the socks and shoes. He'd done well with the sizes. He toweled the boy's hair, popped on the *chapeau* and handed him the bear. When Gilbert saw his reflection in the one long mirror in the shower tent, he danced and smiled, turning round and round, laughing at the little boy in the mirror. Dad bundled up the old clothes in the brown paper.

While Dad showered and changed into a clean uniform, Gilbert kept wiping off the steam so he could stare in the mirror, making faces and turning to see himself from all sides. At dinner, he smiled his shy smile, hiding a little behind Dad, when other officers admired his new clothes.

Later, Dad held Gilbert's hand as he walked him up the path to Madame Bisson's house and handed her the package of the old clothes. She gasped and frowned when she saw Gilbert in his new finery. Gilbert waved from the door and said goodnight.

The next day, however, when Gilbert came down the hill to meet Dad, he was wearing the old worn sweater and tan shorts and looked like he was about to cry. Dad stared at the boy in disbelief.

He handed his clipboard to the next in charge and told him he'd be right back, then took Gilbert's hand and marched back up the hill and rapped on the door. Madame Bisson opened it and scowled. Dad motioned to Gilbert, put his hands on his hips, and narrowed his eyes. Gilbert hid behind Dad.

"*Et où sont les nouveaux vêtements?*" he demanded. And where are the new clothes?

She shrugged, then disappeared into the dark house. When she reappeared, she had the clothes wrapped up in the brown paper again, tied tight with the string.

"*Maintenant, je vous attends.*" Now, I am going to wait, Dad barked, crossing his arms across his chest and tapping his foot. She reached for Gilbert and yanked him into the house. A few moments later, Gilbert reappeared, white-faced but wearing the new clothes and holding tight to the bear.

"*Merci,*" Dad said through clenched teeth and held the boy's hand as they went back down the path to the camp. From that day on, Gilbert appeared each morning wearing his new clothes, with the bear tucked into his pocket or inside his blue sweater.

In late October, the air turned crisp as the days shortened and bright red apples fell off the trees all over Normandy. Cows grazed on the dying grass and farmers gathered what they could from their trampled fields. The area felt again like the peaceful farming region it had been before the invasion. Paris had been liberated August 25th and all the fighting had moved east, pushing the Germans back toward Germany.

Dad had hoped to get a chance to visit the "City of Light" before he left France, but the rebuilding work that the Seabees performed was so much in demand that he never managed to get the leave to go.

His orders had changed and his battalion was leaving, to head back across the English Channel and then to make the long sea voyage home to America. He hid that fact from Gilbert, trying to put off the painful news as long as possible.

But the day of departure, when Gilbert saw Dad's empty tent and wooden sea locker by the door, he burst into tears.

"*Non*," he screamed. "*Non!*"

Dad knelt down and pulled the boy close. Gilbert buried his head in Dad's thick, wool Navy coat, sobbing. Sailors bustled by, laughing and excited to be going home, with heavy sea bags hoisted onto their shoulders. A pair of sailors pulled up in a Jeep and hoisted Dad's locker up.

This was how it had all started, he thought, as he held Gilbert on the dry grass outside his tent. He'd knelt down and met this little guy just four months before. Now Gilbert was a part of his life. As he patted the boy and tried to soothe him, he felt his own tears in the crisp October wind.

"*Sois fort,*" Dad said in a husky voice. Be strong. "*Tu dois être fort maintenant.*" You have to be strong now.

As men hurried by, heading for the ship and home, Dad held Gilbert for as long as he could before the final moment of goodbye.

Part II

1953
Nine Years Later...

3

My father is dreaming. He's thrashing and mumbling and waving his arms. I'm four and am standing by his bed, waiting. It is fall, 1953 and he's been home from the Korean War for a few months. Because it is a Sunday morning, I know he'll read me my special book. I don't know what he is dreaming about, but I sense that he is far away. I touch his shoulder.

"Daddy, will you read me my story?"

I clutch my favorite picture book, *The Golden Egg*, about the duck that hatches out of an egg with a rabbit standing by. I can't read yet, but I've looked at the book so many times that the binding is starting to come apart and the shiny clear paper on the front is peeling off.

Behind me, my parents' two imposing mahogany chests of drawers stand against the sidewall. A large statue of St. Joseph reigns on Dad's dresser, the Virgin Mary on Mom's. On Dad's, there are also a set of keys, coins in a small leather purse and one of my finger paintings from kindergarten—red and blue swirls with a purple heart in the center, my small fingers evident in the movement of the paint.

I love that painting. That was the moment when I discovered that red and blue combined to make purple. I gave it to my daddy and was proud that he had it on his dresser.

He's sleeping in an undershirt and jockey shorts, his usual sleeping attire. I'd seen it sometimes at night, when he got me up to go to the bathroom, patted my back when I was throwing up or comforted me through a nightmare. In summer, when the one-hundred-degree heat made it hard to sleep, he often stood by my bed, raising and lowering the sheet, creating a cool breeze, till I fell back asleep.

"Daddy, will you read me my story?" I touched him again.

He opened his eyes and looked at me, but his glassy eyes looked right through me. He was somewhere else. I waited. We'd done this before. I knew he'd come back to me. He sat up on one arm and shook his head, blinked his eyes, looked around the room and then at me. Then he smiled at me and I could see in his eyes that he was back.

"Of course. Of course I'll read you your story."

He patted the space next to him, stretched, then threw the pillow back so that he could lean on it against the green plastered wall and I could snuggle against his broad chest.

"Sit right here and we'll read your story."

I hopped up, holding my book tight against the front of my faded cotton pajamas with the blue flowers on them. In some vague and undistinguished way, I sensed that I was a link back into this life, a child he loved, from wherever he'd been in his dreams. I didn't know that in the world of his dreams, another child he loved called out to him, reaching out his arms.

I didn't know yet about Gilbert.

I snuggled close, listened and giggled as he acted out the antics of the duck hatching out of the egg, in his deep voice.

26

Then he carried me into the yellow kitchen, jiggling up and down as we walked till I giggled, and set me down at my place at the table for a bowl of Wheaties or Ruskettes. Gradually, everyone wandered in for breakfast before we left for Mass.

In my small world, the yellow kitchen, like the rest of our house, seemed huge. Years later, when I went back to visit, I saw that it wasn't that large. When we first moved in, the walls and cabinets got painted a shiny, cheery yellow.

New linoleum, beige with brown flecks, covered the old pine floors. The hope was that the linoleum pattern might hide the dirt that four children, playing outside all the time tracked in, even with the best of intentions.

We moved to the big old house when my dad was overseas in the Korean War. So crowding into the kitchen together probably made us feel safe, without him with us. Then, throughout my childhood, the kitchen and the yellow Formica table remained the hub of the household and of our lives.

My parents met by chance in 1940, when my father, who was working at his first engineering job in Helena, Montana, happened to go to a dance after a basketball game on a frigid February night. My mother, on a trip from Australia and visiting Helena, also attended that dance.

There must have been a great physical attraction between them to blind them to their differences. It wasn't just their nationalities that set them apart.

My father, born in 1914, the middle of five sons, grew up on a farm in South Dakota and put himself through the South Dakota School of Mines by working nights in a printing shop. His whole life he'd worked hard, going to bed early and getting up early. His mother, a loving, gentle and kind farm wife, cooked, canned, and raised a big vegetable garden and chickens.

My mother was born Daisy Catherine Bonnye Finch in 1915 in Sydney, Australia. A year-and-a-half later her father deserted the family, just before her mother gave birth to a second daughter. My mother grew up being told that her father was dead. Her mother's father, a successful businessman in Melbourne, took care of them. Mom was sent off to a Catholic boarding school at age eight, so spent most of her childhood with nuns. There are photos of her making her debut at eighteen in a long white gown.

When she, her mother and sister made the six-week voyage to America in 1939, they traveled on a luxury liner. She smoked, drank and liked to stay out late partying. When she met my father, she had never made a bed or cooked a meal.

In spite of these differences, or perhaps ignorant of them, after a whirlwind courtship of less than three months my parents were married at the Catholic Church in Missoula, Montana. They are a handsome couple in their wedding photo from that day, innocent of the challenges that lay ahead of them.

But they had problems from the start. My mother had no real experience with men, growing up without a father and being taught by nuns. My father had no sisters, there were no women in his engineering classes and he couldn't have married a woman more unlike his own mother if he had tried.

My brothers, Kenton and Clark, were born in quick succession, then World War II came along. With Dad's training and being overseas, first in Europe and then in the Pacific, the war separated my parents for over two years.

After the war, my sister Sharon and I joined the family, part of the post-war baby boom.

At that point, my mother had four children, ages seven, five, two and a newborn.

There was the washing and ironing, the cooking and cleaning and the shopping. To my dad, all that work would have seemed normal, after what his mother had done on the farm. If my mother complained, he may not have listened with a sympathetic ear.

The tension between my parents was the air that I breathed for as far back as I can remember. My mother was angry with my father and she was angry with me for being close to him. And it got worse over the years. Life felt like a precarious experience. Except when Dad was around. I knew I was safe then.

Dad loved to tell the story of how as a toddler, I'd sit on the front porch of our house and wait for him to walk up the hill from work. Still in diapers, I wore a cotton dress and sturdy leather shoes.

When I'd spot him, I'd jump up and toddle off down the front path, past the brown weeds, which should have been a lawn, and turn right onto the main sidewalk. As I'd head down the hill, my chubby legs picked up speed, going faster and faster. He'd swoop me up into his arms just seconds before I would have toppled over onto the hard cement. When he'd tell me the story, he'd swoop me up again, just like he did then and I'd squeal.

Being the youngest meant I was always the shortest, slowest, least coordinated of the bunch, clamoring to keep up. But when my dad hoisted me up in his strong arms, then I was at his eye level, all six feet two inches of his tall frame, meaning I was not only way higher than my siblings, I was higher than most of the other adults in the room, even my mother.

Dad moved through space with power and speed—later on we'd run to try to keep up. When he carried me, I could move along at his pace—now that was an advantage. I remember how it felt to be held in his arms, close to him like that. Even if he was busy with others, talking, he'd let you know that you were welcome there.

He told me that one time when he was leaving on an airplane, the roar of the propellers frightened me and I clung to him shivering. But when I realized he was getting on the plane, I said, "I'll go with you Daddy."

Just after my third birthday, December 1951, Dad's Seabees unit was called up to go overseas in the Korean War. There's a photo taken on the day he left, in front of our house. He's wearing his dress Khaki uniform and Sharon and I are hanging onto either side of him. I am not smiling. I knew he was going away and what would I do without him?

Then he got into the back seat of a car and the door closed with a thwack. I'd never seen my daddy in the back seat of a car, with someone else driving. He looked out the window and waved as they pulled away. I watched the car disappear down the street until it was gone.

I turned to my sister Sharon, held onto her and cried, the cotton of her school uniform scratching my face. She didn't move away from me, but just let me cry. After a moment, she took my hand to walk away, but I kept staring down the street. Maybe if I stood there long enough, he would come back?

While my father was away overseas, we moved into the large, old house, on three weed-filled acres interspersed with orange, grapefruit, tangerine, lemon and plum trees and surrounded by avocado groves.

The size of the new place made it fun for hide-and-go-seek, with so many rooms to explore. One day, as Sharon and I played, I snuck into my parents' closet to hide. I hid in the farthest corner on Dad's side, tucked in back behind his blue plaid flannel bathrobe that hung down to the floor.

As I waited in the dark, close space, I could hear Sharon counting from one to a hundred. Then her "ready or not, here I come," and the sound of her footsteps on the wood floors as she ran around searching for me.

I waited, scrunched into Dad's robe, breathing in his smells and that of his shaving lotion, Aqua Velva. At first, that felt comforting, the familiar scent of him, there in the closet, from his robe. But then, the next moment, I felt a stab of pain. Oh no, my daddy is *gone. Where is my daddy?*

I pushed aside the clothes, gasping for air and burst out of the closet just as Sharon rounded the corner, her face full of expectation and fun. I threw myself down and curled up into a ball, wailing, "Where is my daddy?" Sharon knelt down next to me, a bit stunned.

"What happened?" she asked.

I sat up and pointed at the closet, a horrified look on my face. "D-D-Daddy's robe, it smells like Daddy," I said, wiping my tears and hiccupping.

"Oh," she said, looking solemn as I flopped down on the floor again, whimpering. She sat close to me and I could see her orange checked shorts out of the corner of my eye and could feel the skin on her bare leg next to my face. It was too hot to go outside in the hundred-degree heat that day and we'd been trying to break up the boredom with this game. She patted my head.

"Yeah, I miss him too. But don't let Mommy hear you. Shh, shhh. She'll be mad, remember?"

I remembered the hard slaps I had received for crying that I missed my daddy. I breathed hard and traced the lines of the hardwood floor with my finger. It was September 1952 and my father had already been gone for a year. I wanted to scream and cry but that would only get me into more trouble. Sharon sat with me till I calmed down.

Dad came back from Japan and Korea the following July 1953. My first memory of him being home was at the Yellow Formica table where he was handing out the gifts he'd brought back for us.

He was *home*. I'd thought maybe that I had imagined his loving presence, warm hugs and deep laugh. But there he was again, calling me Diane Mary, holding me tight and smelling like Dad. I wanted to hang onto him, but knew I'd be in trouble with my mother for that, so sat in my chair and trembled with excitement. I couldn't eat, so pushed my food around on my plate. Luckily, that night, no one noticed.

Sharon got a wind up doll with a pretty pink dress and also a kitten that batted at a just-out-of-reach butterfly, suspended on a wire. I got a wind up, brown, furry monkey that clapped cymbals. There were Japanese comic books, fascinating in their foreignness, and my brothers got shiny bright jackets. We learned to count to ten in Japanese: *Ichi, Nee, San, Shi, Go, Roku, Shichi, Hachi, Kyuu, Juu.*

Dad said we learned in five minutes what it took him months to learn. Dad also brought a set of Noritake china back with him, which became our "good" china that we used for holidays. Mom never liked that china. She didn't come right out and say it, but from her forced smile or pursed lips when she looked at it or talked about it, you could tell. I thought it was very pretty—white with little pink and purple flowers all over it. But she liked English bone china and it was clear that this china, from Japan, was not as good.

4

Mom and Dad had agreed on at least one thing, to raise us in the country. That meant that Dad drove forty-five minutes each way down a two-lane road to the Department of the Navy in San Diego where he worked as a civil engineer. For many years he made the commute on an old Indian motorcycle he bought cheap and restored, taking her apart and putting her back together till she shone and purred.

He was so proud of that motorcycle and called her his "ancient Indian." Even before I could read the big round clock on the wall in the kitchen, I could tell the time each evening by the roar of Dad's motorcycle coming up the driveway.

That was a signal that it was five forty-five, time for Sharon and me to stop playing paper dolls or dress up or to come in from outside and set the table for dinner, with the yellow plastic Melmac dishes and the stainless steel silverware, a white paper napkin folded under each fork.

At six o'clock sharp, our family of six crowded around the yellow Formica table. Dad and Mom sat on each end, my sister across from me at Dad's end, our older brothers next to us, at Mom's end.

The menu rarely changed—meat and potatoes, cooked frozen vegetables, salad with avocado and a whole loaf of bread toasted, to help fill us up. Our glasses of whole milk came from Hollandia Dairy, our local dairy just across town. The milkman left the wire rack of frosty bottles on our back porch three mornings a week. When you popped the cardboard top off the milk bottle, thick cream gleamed on the top. For dessert, there might be canned peaches or fruit cocktail in heavy syrup and sometimes cookies.

But to get dessert, I had to clean my plate. And I hated those frozen vegetables, especially the lima beans. The yellow vinyl and chrome chairs that matched the table had food scrunched into the places where the chrome met the vinyl. Some of that food was my vegetables from previous dinners.

Dad's childhood on the farm during the Great Depression taught him the value of food. He loved to see us eat. At the dinner table, he told the same corny jokes and stories over and over. After dinner, he'd fog up his glasses by blowing steam from his coffee cup, then look around and ask, "Where'd everybody go?" I'd laugh so hard I'd often get the hiccups.

On the nights that we ate chicken, he liked to tell the story of how, when he was a boy, his mother Signe, would pronounce, "Donald, go get me a chicken." This chicken would pay the violin teacher, Miss Larson, for four weeks of Dad's lessons.

Dad had created a little trap with a bent wire, so he could nab a chicken at the neck, lead it off to the side and chop off its head. He didn't like that part, but raising animals for food was a part of farm life. He then walked the mile to the violin teacher's house, with the freshly plucked chicken wrapped in thick, brown paper tucked under one arm and his violin case under the other.

Dad loved his violin lessons, but he had to practice out behind the barn when his father, Bernard, was busy in the fields. Bernard, a powerful man of strong Danish stock, stood 6'4" and thought that violin playing was for sissies.

Signe, who loved music, poetry and books, paid for the lessons with her one source of cash, her chickens. She also sold and bartered her eggs for fabric to make quilts and for store-bought soap that smelled like lavender.

In my mind's eye, I could see my dad, moving the bow across the strings and listening for the notes to sound right as he sent them up to the sky behind the barn. Perhaps his mother heard him as she shelled peas on the porch or busied herself at the stove, cooking large meals for five sons and a husband, all hungry from farm chores. Maybe she smiled at Dad later, letting him know that she had heard his music.

Dad's voice always softened when he talked about his mother and said her name. Signe had only completed the third grade; she was needed on the farm to help with the younger children and the chores. But she could figure out Dad's complicated high-school algebra and math problems when she helped him with his homework.

I could feel my grandmother's strength in Dad's stories, especially in how she went against my grandfather to give Dad those music lessons. Dad even played the violin for me once, the song "Little Red Wing" and I could see from the way that he swayed with the music that the violin still meant something to him.

But then my mom made a snide comment and I watched as he put the violin back into its case, closed it with a snap and put it on the top shelf of the closet. I never saw him take it down again.

Dad talked about how he and his brothers walked to Pioneer School, a rustic one-room schoolhouse where students sat at wooden desks with inkwells in the right-hand corners, used an outhouse for a toilet and carried in wood to stoke the woodstove. Winters in South Dakota get down to thirty degrees below zero. On those days, his mother would hitch up the wagon and drive them to school.

Many times, as Dad overheard the lessons of the classes several years ahead, he'd blurt out the answers, then receive a frown from the teacher. He never learned cursive writing, except to sign his name, but developed a style of fine, neat printing.

Back at the yellow Formica table, Dad used to say, "If you can't eat, you're sick." That was usually true in our house, when the only time you didn't show up at the table to eat was when you were lying sick in bed.

Many nights, during dinner, he talked about his time in France during World War II. "Eat your vegetables. The people in France didn't have enough to eat during the war."

He liked to tell the story about how it upset him that they used to throw out left over food at the Navy camp. He knew that people were hungry nearby—the farmer's fields had all been trampled in the fighting and during war, there were shortages of everything.

"So when it was my turn to be in charge of the mess tent, I loaded up a Jeep with pans of steaming hot meat, vegetables, bread, butter, pies—whatever I could find. Then I drove down the narrow lane from the camp and stopped at a farmhouse, knocked on the door, gave them a pan and said, "*Pour vous.*" For you.

His eyes lit up at this point, remembering what happened next. "Oh, the French people cried, smiled and shook my hand, speaking so fast that I couldn't keep up with their French. But I understood their gratitude."

He'd stop for a moment, take a sip of his coffee, savoring those memories.

"Each night, I went to a different farmhouse and was greeted with such warmth and surprise. I looked forward to that time at the end of the day. It felt like being Santa Claus." That would make me giggle.

"When I no longer had that duty, the next person in charge just started throwing out the food again. I tried to explain what I had done, how easy it was and what a difference it made. But they just looked at me like I was nuts."

He shook his head at that memory. From all the times I listened to that story, I could see it all in my head, Dad in the Jeep with the pans of food, the farmhouses down a narrow lane and the French people, waving their arms in excitement.

A story that always made me laugh was when Dad described how his high-school French teacher had never learned French, and would study to stay a chapter ahead of her students. She'd also never *heard* French and taught them with a mid- western accent, so *sucre*, sugar, came out sounding like *soocray*.

"On a day when I was taking a break from unloading the ships, drinking a cup of coffee and eating a roll, and a Frenchman walked by and nodded, I'd smile and want to try out my French. I'd hold up my sugar packet and say, "*soocray, n'est-ce pas?*" Sugar, right?

Dad always paused there, and I'd hold my breath, knowing what was coming next.

"The poor Frenchman would look puzzled, then peer at the sugar packet and realize that I was trying to say *sucre*. "*Ah oui,*" the man would nod and exclaim—"*oui, sucre!*" Dad would then say it like it should have sounded, kind of like *sookre*.

"Then I'd point to a pad of butter and say, "*la booray, n'est-ce pas?*" The Frenchman would frown, then brighten up and beam, *"oui, le beurre,"* which sounded like *le burr*, and we'd laugh, a moment of understanding between us." I could tell that Dad's French improved greatly from these encounters.

Dad also liked to tell fables, like "Chicken Little," how the mother hen planted and grew the wheat to make the bread, did all the work, with no one helping. Then, when it was time to eat the bread, everyone wanted to share it. I liked those stories too. All Dad's stories lived together in the soft spaces of my imagination, his life on the farm, France, French people and "Chicken Little."

I first heard the story of Gilbert at the yellow Formica table. Dad always said the boy's name with a soft G sound, the way the French said it, *Jeelbear.* Not Gilbert, with a hard G.

He talked about how Gilbert had looked hungry, so he had invited him to eat with him at the officers' mess tent. On rare nights, he talked about how he tried to adopt Gilbert and bring him home to America. But he didn't elaborate on that.

"Clean your plate now, eat your vegetables. You know, Gilbert DesClos didn't have enough to eat during the war. He would have been happy to eat those lima beans."

I stared at the pale green lima beans, cold now because I had pushed them around my plate for so long, hoping to create some kind of magical vortex that they would disappear into. *Poof.* But they didn't disappear. They stared back at me like big, pale green eyes, and my dad would not give up.

"Hold your nose, close your eyes, chew and drink some milk real fast," Sharon suggested. She was keeping me company while the lima beans and I waited each other out. I'd already squished two into the space between the yellow vinyl chair seat and the silver chrome chair back rails. But there were five more left. Dad was firm.

"They're good for you," he said. So I took a breath and ate them up fast, nose held, eyes closed and milk swallowed. "Good job. You may be excused." Dad smiled. I gagged. Sharon giggled. But it was done.

Who was this Gilbert DesClos, the French orphan boy who would have gladly eaten those lima beans? I knew he was different. First of all, he was *French* and that meant that he spoke those soft musical sounds that were not English. He was also different because he wasn't there with us, but was part of the stories that my father told about his time in France, way back before I was even born. So was Gilbert really real?

My father always told the truth, so it must have been true that Gilbert had almost become my brother. But where would we have put him at our very crowded kitchen table? I already had two elder brothers and wasn't so sure I wanted another one. We had two boys and two girls, even numbers. Gilbert would have tilted that over to three and two.

And the idea of another big boy around seemed like too much. They liked to burp loud, tease my sister and me and wrestle and punch each other. No, not another brother. I don't think my mother wanted another child either. She already seemed like she had too many. And she never said anything about Gilbert when Dad talked about him. Her silence seemed to say that she hadn't been that excited about it.

"What happened to Gilbert?" I'd asked. Dad didn't know and the look in his eyes changed when I asked him. His normally sparkly eyes clouded over and he sighed and looked away. I learned not to ask again.

Still I wondered. Gilbert didn't have a Daddy like I did. And he had almost had my daddy. That must have been really hard for that little boy so far away.

I didn't know that it was also hard for my dad, right there at the table with me, telling me to eat my lima beans.

5

Mom had shortened her name to Bonnye Finch Johnson, started a consignment shop called "Bonnye's Outgrown Shop" and was gone on Saturdays. My brothers had jobs working in people's orchards, so Saturdays, Dad was in charge of Sharon and me. We probably had mismatched tops, bottoms and socks, our hair may not have been combed, but oh did we have fun.

Dad always had a long list of things to fix in our 1917 vintage house—and there was plenty to do—old rusty pipes that squirted water and scary looking frayed wires that crisscrossed in the attic. Growing up on a farm, he learned to tinker and knew how to fix anything—cars, houses, plumbing and wiring. I thought all men could fix things.

As Dad worked, Sharon and I stayed close by. If he needed a part for one of his repairs, we all headed off to a junkyard, where he'd search around in rusty bins. Sharon and I would explore through aisles of bathtubs with orange stains around the drains and giant claw feet, and old toilets and sinks on their sides, clustered together like little families.

Since our mother took the car to work, we'd ride behind Dad on his Indian motorcycle for these errands. Sharon would hang onto his back, and I'd hang onto hers, leaning into the curves to the roar of the engine, our hair blowing wildly. The blue sky moved past through the trees like a kaleidoscope, if I turned my head up to look. It was good to feel my dad, sister and me all linked together as we whizzed down Tenth Avenue, turned right onto Juniper Street and then left at the hanging traffic light at Grand Avenue.

Back home, at lunchtime, Dad had a limited cooking repertoire, so lunch was always fried spam sandwiches. Our job was to toast the bread and slather it thick with margarine, while he fried up the spam, which sizzled and popped, splattering grease all over the top of the electric range. Then he'd slide a thick slab of spam onto the bread.

"Spam sandwich, comin' up, hot and juicy and made to order," he would exclaim as he cooked. Then we'd sit together at the yellow Formica table, eating our sandwiches, the grease dripping down our hands and agreeing about how yummy they were.

It was on one of those Saturdays that we spied the small carnival.

"Can we stop, Daddy? Oh look, there's a roller coaster," Sharon said.

I wasn't sure what a roller coaster was but I saw some small cars, kind of like a train. I liked toy trains.

"Okay, sure we can stop, for a treat," he said. He pulled the Indian motorcycle over and parked.

In the seat next to Sharon on the little train, I saw the hill up ahead. *Uh oh.* The man took our tickets.

Dad stood by the fence, smiling and waving as the train started to move. We edged up the hill, click, click, click, click, then were at the top of the hill and I could see ahead. *Oh no, what was this?* We headed down.

Sharon squealed with delight, but I shuddered and shrieked, hiding my head on her shoulder. As we raced past

Daddy, a blur against the sky and trees, I screamed "Daddy get me offff!" And then he was gone.

Click, click, click, click. I looked back, my face white with fear and my voice high-pitched, "Daddy, get me off!" We headed down the hill again and around back towards the man with the big metal crank that turned the ride on and off, and Daddy.

As we sped by him again, I saw Daddy talking to the man, in a loud voice and waving his arms. I heard "right now" as the train car rushed past again, then the loud screech of brakes and we were stopping, just short of the hill. By this time I was huddled into Sharon's side. Then Daddy was standing there, holding out his arms.

"It's all right. I've got you."

He lifted me up and out and to the other side of the fence. The man turned the big crank and the train started again. I stood next to Daddy and hid my head into his pants leg and plugged my ears against the sound.

Sharon whizzed by, a blur of excited screams and smiles. Daddy patted my head, then knelt down and put his arms around me. I shuddered with relief that I was safe from that monster climbing up and barreling back down the hill.

At night, after putting on my cotton J.C. Penney pajamas and brushing my teeth, I'd climb into my single bed, pulling the pink, cotton quilt from my grandma Signe up around my neck. I'd only met that grandma once, but felt her caring through all those hand-stitched threads in my quilt and where she'd signed her name in dark pink thread, *Signe Johnson, 1954.*

Sharon's bed was a few feet away from mine, but my bed was against the outside wall. I scrunched up against the cold plaster, trying to hide under the windowsill. That way, when the boogieman looked in, he wouldn't see me. He would see Sharon and that worried me, but I didn't know what to do about that. I'd already checked under the bed to make sure there were no monsters hiding there. It was all clear, for now.

One night, I lay awake, tense and restless; Sharon was already asleep. I chewed on my fingernails until they hurt. That was going to get me into more trouble with my mother, but I couldn't seem to stop. I hugged my teddy bear tight and squeezed my eyes shut, hoping that would bring sleep.

When I woke up later, the house was quiet, which made the scratching on the window just above me that much louder. I could hear Sharon's quiet breathing in the next bed, then the scratching. I shivered. Should I look? What was doing that scratching? When I sat up to look, I saw a monkey at the window, looking right in at me and screamed out, in terror.

"Daddy, Daddy, there's a monkey at the window!"

I yelled as loud as I could, then covered my head with my quilt, so the monkey couldn't see me. I heard Daddy's footsteps coming down the hall, then the squeak of my bed springs and felt the sag of my mattress when he sat down on the edge of the bed. I heard his soothing, calm voice through the covers.

"Shhh, shhh, what's the matter Diane Mary?"

"There's a monkey at the window, scratching the glass," I whimpered. "I saw it, looking at me."

"Come on out now and let's look," he said.

I peeked out from under the quilt. He smiled at me and pointed to the window.

"No monkey, see? Just tree branches and leaves scratching the glass. Go back to sleep now. No reason to be scared."

He patted my back and sat with me as if he had all the time in the world. He acted like it didn't matter that I'd awakened him in the middle of the night for an imaginary monkey at the window. I went back to sleep feeling safe, at least for that moment.

During the day, I loved to run and play, skip and whoop, thrilled to feel my heart beating fast and my muscles getting stronger as I grew, able to keep up better with my sister and brothers.

One day, coming home from playing hard with a friend, I stuck my sweaty head out the back, side window of the pink 1950 Studebaker. The cool breeze on my damp forehead and scalp sent a thrill through my body.

I also loved to breathe in the fresh air and not my mother's cigarette smoke, which filled up the car. Then the sharp reprimand and my head yanked hard back into the car, with a slap on the arm.

"You're going to catch pneumonia doing that. Close that window now," my mother snapped, from the front seat. I cranked the window back up and watched as my body heat steamed it up in seconds.

Who cares, I thought, as I drew faces on the steamy glass. And what is p'monia anyway? I just want to feel that fresh air.

I was so sick that I couldn't get out of bed. The doctor came to visit with his stethoscope and black bag, then shook his head and talked in a low tone to my parents. Sharon peeked around the corner. I was not getting better. I was just so hot.

I don't remember being transferred to the hospital, but would wake up sometimes when a nurse would try to get me to drink something. At night, I could sense Dad sitting with me, but was always too tired to talk to him. One night, his voice pierced through my stupor and I heard him pleading with the doctor and nurses.

"You've got to do something. You can't just let her lie there."

"There is one new drug, but it is experimental," the doctor said.

"Use it. Do it now," he thundered.

I knew he was there, trying to pull me back from where I was floating away to. A little later, they helped me to sit up to swallow a pill, then I fell back into the bed.

"It could take some time for it to take effect," the doctor said.

I could just make out my dad in the chair next to the bed as I drifted off again. The voices and my dad seemed so far away, but I could feel him there with me.

When I woke up again, I was hovering above the bed. I could see the hospital room, the single metal bed, the wood floors, and the table with the glass of orange juice with the red plastic bendy straw. My father sat in the metal chair and his head dropped forward every few seconds, then jerked back up, then down again. It was the middle of the night and he was dozing.

I saw my small, unmoving body, showing barely a bulge in the bed. But wait. I was up above that bed, looking down. And I felt like I was drifting away, being pulled by an invisible tide.

It felt all dreamy, cocoon-like and warm, but different from the feverish heat in my body. Soft, blurry even. I saw a glow behind me and then I looked back at my daddy. He was there, along with the lump in the bed and that glow beyond the hospital wall. I was floating right through the wall, so easy, toward that golden glow.

But wait. Stop. Hold on just a minute. I was *leaving* through that wall. I couldn't leave through a wall. Something was really wrong here.

I looked back at my daddy, nodding forward again and thought of sitting in his lap, looking at a book, or having a piggy-back ride when I could hear the change jingle in his pants pocket.

But this floating. Did this mean that I was dying? I had heard about dying, where people go away and don't come back. A little girl in my class drowned in a boating accident; she was there on Friday and didn't come back on Monday. She never came back. Maybe this is where they went, toward that yellow glow on the other side of the wall, where I was going.

I felt so free. It would be so easy. But what about my daddy? He would be so sad. He would never forget that I had died. I looked back at him again in the metal chair.

And wait. I'm only eight years old. I don't want to die.

I opened my eyes and blinked at the bright sun shining through the window of my hospital room. I wiggled in the narrow iron bed and felt the starched white sheet against my thin bare legs. A nice young nurse was looking down at me, smiling and her eyes were very bright blue and filled up with water.

"There you are now. There you are. Welcome back."

Her voice sounded husky and she brushed my cheek with her soft hand. My throat felt so dry that the insides of my mouth stuck together and I couldn't talk.

"Here, I brought you some nice cold orange juice. It will make you feel better and help you to get strong again."

She held it out for me and helped me to sit up. I drank a few sips, swallowing carefully as the dryness eased.

I laid my head back down on the pillow feeling very tired and closed my eyes. I'd had the strangest dream. Daddy was in it and a golden light. I'd been floating away, through that wall over there.

But now I was back. It felt like I'd been gone a long time. The nice nurse said that I'd had pneumonia and had been in the hospital for more than a week.

When I heard the word "p'monia," my stomach clenched tight. I would be in trouble with my mother. It would be my fault for sticking my head out of the window.

For the p'monia.

6

My mother sold her outgrown shop and began working at a travel agency, which allowed her to earn a free ticket to Australia. In the summer of 1957, she was returning to her country for the first time since 1939 and bringing back her mother, Nana Daisy, to stay with us.

Dad took that chance to pack up all four kids to travel across the country to his family reunion over the 4th of July in South Dakota. He'd only gone back a few times since he left in the late 1930's and we kids had never been.

We had a Lincoln Capri, a long, sleek white car that Dad had bought used. Whenever we needed a "new" car, he disappeared for the day, returning with a different car at day's end, one he could pay cash for with the trade-in. Mom was never pleased with his purchase. She wanted a new car.

The day he came home with the Lincoln Capri, I went out to look and passed Mom on her way back to the house, scowling and taking fierce puffs on her cigarette. I missed what she had said to Dad, but could see the effect of her words.

He stood by the car with his head down, staring at the ground. I climbed into the back seat and jumped up and down while Sharon slid in on the other side.

"Oh Dad, nice soft seats. And electric windows—can I try?" He turned the engine on and Sharon and I each made our windows go up and down, amazed at the "whir" sound that meant that the window was moving without someone cranking it hard.

"We'll have a lot more room in this car, for all six of us. We won't be so crammed," I added.

Dad smiled at our excitement. When it was time to make the trip to South Dakota, he took out the back seat, laid our old, mismatched and scratched suitcases down, then put a worn, pinstriped mattress on top, covered with a faded sheet. Sharon and I were to have the back seat, with Dad and the boys up front.

My two brothers were fifteen and thirteen and excited about being able to drive some on the long stretches across the country, away from towns—and cops. Sharon and I settled in with three comic books and some pillows on the mattress.

Dad figured out our route so that we stopped and camped in National Parks, like Yosemite, Bryce Canyon, and Yellowstone. In the trunk, a green, tattered, canvas army tent, five army-issue down sleeping bags and five air mattresses got stashed.

When we stopped for the night, ropes, stakes, poles and canvas turned into a tent, then Dad and my brothers raced each other to blow up the air mattresses. At dark, we all crawled in and squished together.

I discovered the wonder of Yosemite, my first time ever seeing a rushing river, huge granite cliffs, and pine trees reaching high into the sky. We swam in the icy cold river, shivering next to the campfire after to get warm, but excited and happy. Each day we arrived at a new place to explore, even if it was only for one night.

Dad handled meals by streamlining the process. Dinner was Dinty Moore Beef Stew heated in the can over the open fire, served in tin cups. Breakfast, those same tin cups appeared, with canned milk diluted with water, poured over Wheaties. Sharon and I complained loudly, especially when the menu didn't change from day to day. But we were so hungry we had to eat it. That was all there was.

Lunch consisted of sandwiches made along the side of the road, peanut butter and jelly, or sometimes a package of lunchmeat gobbled up in one sitting. We didn't have a cooler. Food preparation was not Dad's strong suit.

The sun burned through the back windows of the Lincoln Capri, and the hours dragged by. Sharon and I got bored back there rolling around on the old mattress.

But my small world expanded day by day in the National Parks, with the scent of pine trees, fresh mountain air, and the sound of a river rushing by. Even the stinky geysers at Yellowstone where I clung onto Dad, afraid I'd fall into those bubbling pools, were interesting and exciting. Dad had never seen the National Parks either, so he relished the experiences too.

On the last day we drove and drove, pulling into my grandparents' farm late at night. Over the next week, we met aunts, uncles, cousins, and even my ninety-year-old great-grandfather. The sixteen cousins ranged in age from babies to teens with Sharon and me in the middle at ten and eight. The adults sat around visiting, and we kids raced past, playing tag or hide-and-go-seek. We all lined up for the group photos, the shortest in front.

I loved the organized chaos of it and so many people who felt like my dad, warm and openhearted. It felt special to see where he had grown up, to sleep in the room he slept in as a child and to be with his mother and father, on the farm. I'd met them once or twice, but only at our home, where there was an unspoken tension and strain with my mother.

Here, people laughed and told stories and they loved my dad. At home, Dad went by Don or D.K., but his family called him Donald. Dad and his brothers lined up with their arms around each other for special photos of the "boys." Dad's youngest brother Lester had died in a plane crash five years earlier. There were choked voices, even some tears, at all being together again, without him.

Sometimes, as I'd race through, one of them would grab me and exclaim, "Oh Donald, she's just like you." Those words felt good in my ears and in my heart.

My grandma Signe stood 5'1" tall, tiny next to grandpa Bernard who was even taller than my dad. Grandma wore a flowered cotton housedress, a white apron, and sturdy black shoes, with her gray hair tied up in a bun. I was already almost as tall as she was.

I crept downstairs into her cellar one day and when my eyes became accustomed to the dark, saw shelves and shelves lined with quart and half-gallon mason jars filled with fruits and vegetables. There were loaves of fresh-baked breads and pies lined up like a bakery. She must have worked for months to get ready for this reunion.

Grandma Signe didn't say much to me, but the look in her eyes was soft and gentle. She loved to grow flowers, in addition to tending her huge vegetable garden, her chickens and her cats.

After our visit to the farm, we faced the long ride home, the boredom in the car and more camping. My brothers drove and Sharon and I read comics as America passed by the windows of the Lincoln Capri. But I'd learned that I had a whole family of warm and loving people, just like my dad, who thought I was special. I'd felt the warmth of my grandmother's love. I tucked it all away inside of my heart.

My mother returned from Australia with her mother, Nana Daisy Finch, a short, stout, gray-haired woman who smelled like baby powder, wore a corset and spoke with such a strong Australian accent that we barely understood her. Her presence added to the already busy and chaotic household.

Dad still rode his motorcycle to his job in San Diego each day. I remember one night going out to meet him in a drizzle. I heard the roar, meaning he was coming up the driveway and watched, as the single headlight got closer in the dark, wet night. The rain streamed off his bright yellow rain suit as he pulled in and parked.

When he got off and turned towards me, the way that he stood and the look in his eyes seemed peaceful and invigorated. He must have loved those forty-five minutes each way, alone with his thoughts, the wind roaring past, the sun coming up in the morning or the hills becoming shadows as the sky turned dark in the evening.

It was his time away from the chaos of four boisterous children, one angry wife and now her mother. Dad still told his stories at dinner, about France, the war and Gilbert, and I felt comforted by the familiarity of it all, even though so many other things were changing around me.

Part III

1961

7

Sharon and her best friend Holly huddled close together on Sharon's bed discussing their first day of high school, fall 1961. I was still in the eighth grade, eager to hear about their new world. They talked about all their classes—biology, chemistry, and for Holly, French I. Sharon had to take Latin. My mother insisted that it was the "mother of all languages" and that we all had to take two years. Mass was also still said in Latin. Sharon read from her Latin I book. I was unmoved.

Then Holly began reading from her French I book, words and phrases like *chambre meublée*—furnished room. She tilted her head and made her lips into a kissing shape, "*Oui, oui, chambre meublée.*" She and Sharon giggled; I was transfixed.

It sounded exciting, hypnotic and worldly to be able to make those French sounds. Holly said, "*Je t'aime.*" I love you. I sighed. How romantic. I kept listening, my attention riveted on the sounds and on my own sense of excitement.

I'd heard French words before, when Dad talked about his time in France during the war, but Dad's French sounded Midwestern, American, boring. This French sounded luscious, sensual, inviting.

That day, that moment, those sounds, may not be something that Sharon nor Holly would even remember. But as I sat there, on the soft chenille bedspread in the bedroom of my childhood, something inside of me woke up and paid attention.

I could learn those sounds and words and be a part of that place in the French I textbook, with the side walk cafés where starving artist types sipped strong coffee out of tiny cups. I didn't know what starving artists were and I had never tasted coffee, but I sensed that if I went to this place, where they said *chambre meublée* like that, I could be happy.

I could also be far away from the small town where I'd lived my whole life, far away from my mother's coldness and anger. I could even visit some of the places Dad had been during the war. If I learned French, I could disappear into this country with the Eiffel Tower and castles. It seemed like a fairy tale and a fairy tale sounded good right then.

The next year, my freshman year at high school, I suffered through the dreaded Latin I class—*amo, amas, amat, amamus, amatis, amant*, the conjugation of the verb 'love' in Latin. I was unmoved. The teacher, Mrs. Vogel, had taught both my brothers and Sharon and looked like she was old enough to remember the days when they still *spoke* Latin. I had the class right after lunch and struggled to stay awake.

I longed to study French. My best friend Susan had started German and I so envied her learning a *real* language. I had never forgotten my excitement that day on the bedspread when Holly had read out the French words. I wanted those sounds. So I begged, pleaded and cajoled my mother into letting me out of Latin after only one year.

"I could take French," I argued, a language that people still spoke. Didn't that make more sense? My mother actually listened to me and I prevailed. I could start French my sophomore year. Goodbye to Latin forever! I couldn't wait.

The next year, Sharon and I began French I together; I was a sophomore, she was a junior. It was a first for us to share a class, and we sat next to each other, and chatted before class. But once the bell rang, I was riveted on the French. That first year, our egotistical teacher enjoyed hearing himself speak French in a pompous manner, but gave an easy A or B if you were a girl and smiled at him. I did smile, but also earned my A+.

My junior year, my second year of French, Sharon and I moved into Mr. Maiwald's class. He was a short German man with a pointed head and one eye that didn't move. He also had the reputation of being the hardest teacher in the school, and flunked students regularly. Next to my dad, he was the smartest person I'd ever met.

Mr. Maiwald made it very clear on the first day that he would give hard tests, be a tough grader, but that we would learn French. I was thrilled. I became obsessed. I made flash cards by writing French vocabulary words onto "3x5" index cards and carried them with me wherever I went. I studied them on the half-hour bus ride to and from school.

I put them on the ironing board so I could learn new words when I ironed my starched white gym shirt and dark blue gym shorts each week or the blouses with the big ruffles down the front. I stayed up late studying and figuring out all the tiny nuances of how the verb endings had to agree when you conjugated them, all of the different tenses, all the accents and irregular verbs. I knew he was going to ask those things on the exams. But it wasn't that. I had to learn it all for myself.

French and my dream of going to France became the center of my own private universe. In it, I was safe from my real life as a teenager, from problems with my mother, from boyfriend woes, from worrying if I was fat. When I said those sounds in my head to an imaginary French person, *"Bonjour, je m'appelle Diane,"* Hello, my name is Diane, I felt free and alive.

I scored 100% on all the tests. It became a sort of silent battle between us, this short, stocky German man with one funny eye and this tall, shy, high school coed. He wanted to see if he could make me stumble. He never did.

Excelling in his class felt exhilarating. Each word I learned, each rule I mastered, and each *accent aigu* or *accent grave* I correctly placed on a French word became a small victory. It took me another step closer to my dream of flying across the Atlantic Ocean to France, sitting at one of those sidewalk cafés and moving my lips like a kiss to speak French.

My senior year, in French III, I worked harder than ever. Mr. Maiwald spoke only French in class, so I was good at understanding but still shy about speaking it.

The big house felt empty with my sister away at college and my brothers grown up and gone. By this time, my mother barely talked to my father. She had moved into my brothers' empty bedroom at the other end of the house.

The three of us still sat down to dinner most nights at the yellow Formica table, eating food that I prepared when I got home from school. One night stands out in my memory.

During the mostly silent meal, as our knives and forks scraped against the yellow Melmac dishes, I heard my father sigh and glanced up at him. I noticed his plastic pocket liner in his shirt with his pen and slide rule sticking out; he had just come home from work. Then I looked at his face. His normally bright blue eyes looked dull and his shoulders slumped. He looked so lonely and sad.

He'd asked me about my day and I'd answered, "fine." But after I looked at him, I decided to break the heavy and awkward silence in the room and tell him about my day.

"French class was good, today, Dad."

His looked up at me. His face brightened.

"Mr. Maiwald gave a really hard test but I don't think I missed any. I answered all the tricky questions and I wonder if that makes him happy or mad, but I'm guessing happy. I love learning French and someday I want to go and live in France."

"Oh, that's grand," Dad said. He loved the word grand. Or "Wouldn't that beat all," he liked to say, too, when something seemed unusual or special.

I could feel my mother's cold glare. Somehow, I was breaking an unspoken rule, but I didn't care. I couldn't turn away from my dad any longer.

"We're learning about World War II in history class, Dad," I said, pushing my plate to one side. "You were in that Normandy Invasion, right? And all your stories, about the French people and the orphan Gilbert you wanted to adopt— that all happened when you were there, right?"

"Yes, that's right." He sat up straighter. "We was over there in France for almost five months." Dad sometimes used "we was" when he got caught up in an emotional story. His parents, Scandinavian farmers who spoke with strong accents and not always the best English grammar, used that expression. I took a sip of milk.

"A lot of people died in that war, it sounds like. That must have been awful," I said.

"Yes, wars are always awful," he said and looked down. The frown line in his forehead deepened and when he ran his hands through his short, crew cut hair, I noticed how much it was graying around his temples.

As Dad and I chatted more about French and what I was learning, he told his story again about how his French teacher's accent was so terrible that *merci beaucoup* came out sounding like "mercy buttercups." I always laughed when he talked about his French teacher, especially now that I was learning French.

"And with Gilbert—you spoke French with him, right?"

"Oh yes." Dad's eyes softened. It was as if he was watching a movie that only he could see. "Gilbert didn't know any English, though he learned a few words while we was there."

My mother had lit a cigarette. The smoke curled over her head and headed towards me. I heard her sharp inhale and the scrape of the metal legs of her chair against the linoleum as she stood up to leave. A moment later, the door to her room slammed behind her.

Dad sat drinking his coffee while I cleared the table and stacked the rest of the dishes in the sink. As I came back to wipe the table with the gray dishrag he started talking again.

"You know how you said you are learning about the Normandy invasion?"

"Yes," I said.

"Well I was assigned to go in on "D-Day plus one," as they called it, the day after D-Day. It was the luck of the draw. On June 6th, I was on a Navy ship just back from the coast. Those poor men who landed that morning on Omaha Beach, one of the American landing beaches, the Germans mowed them down."

His eyes looked glassy now and he spoke softly, almost to himself, looking down at his coffee mug. I slipped back into my chair and leaned forward to listen, pushing the old dishrag aside. This was not at all like the other stories he'd told about his time in France.

"Something went wrong. Because of the cloud cover, the planes that flew over just before dawn missed their targets. The men pouring out of the landing crafts, trying to run to the beach kept falling down, cut down by German bullets. It was a massacre."

He stared straight ahead now, not seeing me at all. He'd set down his coffee mug but was gripping it hard. "Finally, one of the Navy destroyers, without orders—but the captain did the right thing for sure—pulled in close, firing over the heads of the men on the beach and blasting the cliffs. That and a few brave men, who made it up the hill and blew up the German bunkers, made it safer. But that was after hours and hours of slaughter."

He was holding onto his coffee mug so hard that his knuckles had turned white.

"I lost friends, other officers, and men I'd trained with and worked with for over a year, gone. Such a waste of human life in a few hours on that beach."

His eyes filled with tears.

"The next day, when I landed, the sea was red with the blood of all those young men, thousands of them dead. I'll never forget that scene."

Tears streamed down his face. I'd never seen my father cry. I reached over and touched his hand.

"Oh Dad, I am so sorry."

He looked up, startled. We sat in silence. He wiped the tears away with his white paper napkin and cleared his throat, trying to compose himself. His hand shook as he raised his coffee mug to take a sip.

I stared at the yellow Formica table and the old dishrag that had gathered up some crumbs and watched him out of the corner of my eye. This person, my father, who helped me with my math homework and handed out my three-dollar allowance each week, had seen so many things, far beyond the scope of what I could imagine.

He was a separate person who had a life before I was born and knew of things I could never know, horrors, in this case, of a war I'd only just read about in a history book. He'd been there, in the middle of it, facing his own death and witnessing the death of all those young men.

I felt renewed love and respect for him and a bit of awe. What else didn't I know about him?

He passed something on to me that night, something unsaid about life and experience. He showed me how there are moments in each person's life after which nothing can ever be the same.

8

At the end of the following summer, I attended a five-day freshman orientation at UCLA, then caught the train for the two-hour trip back home. My summer boyfriend Doug was going to meet me. I was seventeen.

At ten o'clock, the train screeched to a stop in the dark, deserted station and Doug was waiting, just like he'd promised. I hugged him and felt relieved to have survived my first solitary adventure out in the world.

As we turned to go, I happened to glance down the tracks, and saw my dad, barely visible under the glow of a streetlight. He was there making sure I wasn't left alone at the train station at night. I waved, touched.

He waved back, his typical high wave that resembled a salute, just before he disappeared back into the shadows.

I didn't know that soon, my Dad would no longer be there, to make sure I was okay. At that moment, it was still a normal part of my life, something I almost took for granted. Almost.

A week later, I began at UCLA, trying to find my way around the campus of thirty thousand students. Back in my hometown, population twenty thousand, where many of my kindergarten classmates and I had graduated from high school together, I felt stifled, but also secure in who I was, one of the "Johnson girls," an honor student, respected. UCLA felt cold and intimidating.

I had tested into French III and thought I could handle it. A much better idea would have been to go back to French II, to have a chance to get my feet under me and ease in. But I didn't ease in. It felt like I was dropped into the deep ocean and barely knew how to dog paddle.

We were reading *L'Étranger, The Stranger*, an Albert Camus text that, as far as I could figure out, was about a man who had murdered another man for no clear reason, was in prison and sentenced to death. The reading was confusing, depressing and I didn't even want to study it.

But the worst part was that my identity as the brilliant French student, the best in my school, sank fast. Excelling in French was how I knew I had a place in the world. I was so insecure and shy in every other way, but I did well in French.

Not at UCLA. I cried a lot that first quarter and didn't study much. I earned a C in French III, my first ever grade in French that wasn't an A+. I never understood what happened to *L'Étranger,* sitting in his prison cell. I think they chopped off his head.

In high school, I had enjoyed writing and did well in English classes. But in my freshman English composition class, the teaching assistant wrote all over my papers with red ink and graded them as C-. Another piece of my self-confidence shot down, another area of failure. I decided then and there to avoid writing and to never take an English class again.

Back at home, my parents separated and my father moved into a trailer on our property. They didn't say anything about it, just acted like nothing was different. I didn't have the tools to speak up to them and ask what was going on, but felt confused and sad, which didn't help with my studies.

All that first year, I struggled with the French classes, barely coping, getting B's and C's, getting by. The next summer Dad announced that he was accepting a promotion and moving to Hawaii. In 1967, before cell phones and Skype, he might as well have said he was moving to the moon. At the end of the summer, after I finished my summer job, I was able to travel with him for free as a dependent and spent three idyllic weeks enjoying both Hawaii and the precious time alone with Dad.

One night at dinner, we sat in a booth enjoying some Hawaiian food and chatting about all the new and fun things we were discovering being there. Dad got quiet and I knew he wanted to say something.

"You know Diane Mary, I'm very excited about my new job and about being here. But I want you to know that of all the things that I have accomplished in my life, having a family has been the most important thing. Being a father has been the most important part of my life."

Hawaiian music played in the background and tourists in bright flowered shirts walked by in the restaurant. But at that moment, I felt like I was in a bubble with just my father. My dad was starting completely over, in a new place and life as a single man. But there was no question that first and foremost, he was my dad.

Just before I left to fly back to California, Dad wanted to buy me something special as a souvenir. I picked out a bathing suit and matching top which I had been admiring at the International Market Place, but unable to afford on my own. I cherished having his gift to wear, to remember him and those weeks in Hawaii together.

Then it was time to say goodbye. Another young woman, also headed back to the mainland to college, boarded with me. I walked up the outside stairs to the airplane and turned at the top to look back and wave at Dad.

He stood at the gate and waved back, then didn't budge while the plane taxied down the runway. I could see him out the small window, standing there, in his bright colored Aloha shirt, all by himself.

He got smaller and smaller, then the plane turned and I couldn't see him anymore. I wiped away tears and tried to clear the emotions out of my tight throat as my new friend chatted about college and boys.

The three weeks had been so easy, so fun, so special. I felt happy for Dad and his new life.

But what would I do without him, so far away?

I began my sophomore year at UCLA, still challenged by the French classes, still trembling at writing papers.

My dream of doing my junior year abroad in France the next year felt out of reach. I didn't have the grade point average and if I could somehow get in, how would I pay for it? In the midst of all this turmoil, I met a new boyfriend who gave me a piece of that safe feeling I had lost when Dad moved away.

I missed my Dad. I never talked to him except on rare Sundays when we'd have a hurried phone conversation. He wrote letters, at least once a month, when he sent me a hundred-dollar check to help with expenses. But I wasn't very good at writing back. What could I say? "I'm not doing well in French—too far behind now to ever catch up. I have a new boyfriend." Everything I thought of saying would worry him, so I rarely wrote.

Life seemed so challenging and, feeling confused and rebellious, I turned away from my strict Catholic upbringing, going against all the rules I'd been taught for eighteen years. By spring, I was pregnant. I would not be spending my junior year abroad in France. I would be married, moving to San Francisco and having a baby.

A part of me was excited to be embarking on a new life, moving to a new city, married with a baby. That's what we girls were told was our destiny, after all, to be wives and mothers. But my secret, private part, the French part, mourned the loss of something that I'd cherished for more than five years, a quarter of my young life.

What will become of us, it whispered to me, as I watched bright purple stretch marks zigzag across my ever enlarging stomach each week.

I had experienced my first failure to achieve something I had longed for. It was as if a wave had carried my dream out to sea. I could still see it bobbing in the ocean, but stood helpless on the shore, with no way of reaching it. Its pull had no logical explanation in my real life, but I sensed it, like an underground stream that fed and nourished me.

Then my daughter came into the world, calm and peaceful, looking around with big, wide eyes. I held her in my arms and felt awe that my young body had created this perfect new life. As I cared for her, alone in the apartment, I could feel my father's love guiding me. It felt like a lifeline, something good and pure, from his heart, to mine, to my daughter's and it kept me afloat, it kept me going.

But I missed who I'd been and who I'd wanted to be, that free young woman who'd dreamed of going off to France. My best friend Susan was doing her year abroad in Germany and I'd receive postcards of her adventures in

Europe in the mailbox on my way to the Laundromat. I'd study those postcards of some castle along a river or a famous city I'd remember from a geography lesson as I'd watch a load of cloth diapers spinning in the dryer.

Then my baby daughter would gurgle and smile at me from her stroller and pull me back into real life, my life. Europe and France were a dream world of famous places and night trains through mysterious cities, with no Laundromats in sight. But they were not my world. Those dreams had gotten buried, just like the overdue library books, under stacks of clean cloth diapers.

But I couldn't let go of my love of French. When I'd push my daughter in her stroller at Fisherman's Wharf, if I heard French tourists chatting, I'd dawdle, lean in and listen. I'd buy and cherish a French Vogue magazine then spend hours with my worn French dictionary to decipher the meaning of the many words I didn't know. When I made friends with a young French student, I experienced the thrill of speaking the language again and felt amazed at how much I still remembered.

9

Four years after I left, I returned to UCLA as a focused and determined student who dropped her three-year-old off at daycare on the way. I studied hard and earned A's for my efforts. I felt that my French was too rusty to be my major, but discovered Cultural Anthropology, with classes in both psychology and anthropology. Required to write long papers, I rediscovered my love for and ability in writing.

My dad had remarried and during that time, he and his wife Aileen stopped in for a visit on their way back from a trip to Europe, including some time in France. Dad had waited so long to go back to France; it had been almost thirty years since he was there in 1944.

We were sitting at my kitchen table drinking coffee and chatting when he got quiet and I could tell that he wanted to tell me something. So I waited, looking out the window to the sweet peas I'd planted along a fence. Dad blew on his coffee, took a sip and set down his mug.

"Do you remember how I used to talk about the orphan, Gilbert DesClos, who I tried to adopt and bring back to America?"

"Yes, I do remember your stories about Gilbert," I answered.

"Well, when we were in France, I was so hoping that we could get over to Normandy and I could look for him. We had one day free from the tour, so I had planned to take a train or a bus for the two-hour trip over to the coast. But then Aileen got sick and we had to spend that time seeing doctors." He stared down at his coffee mug and then looked straight ahead.

"I felt so frustrated. Here I was finally back in France, in Paris, wanting to get to Normandy to try to find Gilbert. Then I remembered that during the war, I'd been in Normandy, with Gilbert, wanting to get to Paris." He shook his head.

"Isn't life strange, sometimes?"

I nodded. He went on.

"So, I thought, okay, I'll at least try to call him. I went into a phone booth and began to search through the names in the thick phone book. But I couldn't for the life of me remember how he spelled his name. Was it Du Clos or DesClos?"

"I found some people with both last names, then realized that I was looking in the Paris book, not the Normandy one, and that I'd never find the number there. I stepped out onto the sidewalk and stopped several people who were rushing by, hoping to get some help with my search. I tried to use my high-school French, but the Parisians just shook their heads, not understanding. I had to give up."

He frowned, stared at his mug and sighed. I noticed the wrinkles around his eyes and how gray his hair had become since all those years ago when I'd sat with him, talking about Gilbert.

I hadn't thought about those stories from my childhood in a while, about France and the war and the orphan Gilbert. It was like they'd been put away with my childhood dolls and fairy tale books, a part of my life that was over but not entirely forgotten.

But I noted how even though almost thirty years had passed since Dad had been in France with Gilbert, Dad had not given up on finding him again.

"Dad, I am so sorry. That must have been frustrating. Too bad you couldn't have asked someone with the tour company to try to help you."

He looked up at me. "Oh, I didn't think of that. I should have done that. You're always so resourceful."

"Thanks Dad, I wish I could have helped you somehow." I patted his hand. "Maybe you'll get another chance to try to find him."

Dad nodded and looked at me.

"Yes, maybe so."

My father never traveled back to France for another chance to look for Gilbert.

I only saw Dad every few years for short visits. But just after graduation, and the birth of my second daughter, my husband and I bought a fixer-upper house. Dad was so concerned about all the work involved that he called and announced that he was taking his retirement early so that he could come and help out for a month with the new house. That was the best news I'd heard in a long time. When Dad arrived, we made a list of things that needed doing, prioritizing it.

"Now every day, I want you to take a rest," he insisted.

No problem, I thought. He fixed the clogged plumbing, buying two huge red pipe wrenches, saying they were a gift to us for our new home. Over twenty years later, alone on my property with a broken water pipe gushing like a fountain, I'd dig out those old wrenches and bless him.

He painted, plastered, and cleaned, working steadily every day, just stopping for lunch and dinner. I marveled at his skills and so appreciated his kind spirit there with us. His presence was so comforting. I did rest many afternoons and felt my strength coming back.

When his month was over and he had to head home, I cried. What would I do without him? The house was so empty and though we'd made huge progress, there was so much left to do.

During those years in L.A., of fixing up that house and caring for my daughters, I attended an evening French conversation class held in a woman's home, once a week for six weeks. We sipped French wine, nibbled hors d'oeuvres and chatted in French. It was the first French class I'd taken in over seven years.

I looked forward to that two-hour class all week, relishing the sound of French again, struggling sometimes to recall words and phrases, but remembering a lot and understanding most of what was said. It was my two hours a week to dress up and feel like my old self again, with something precious of my own.

A part of me woke up in that class. I was high for hours and even days afterwards, hearing French echoing in my brain as I hung wet diapers out on the line, did a sink full of dirty dishes or read a bedtime story. French became my private world again where all things were possible and the problems of normal life didn't exist. In that world, the sense of who I was deep down felt like a lifeline and I held on tight.

When we moved from Los Angeles to a new town, one of the first things I did was to sign up for more French classes at the community college. Those hours in the French class fueled me for all the shopping, errands and busyness that filled the rest of my life. I became friends with the French teacher and my daughters and I spent time with her and her two sons, who were bilingual.

I also completed two journalism classes, hoping to find a way to channel my love of writing into a job out in the world. The teacher encouraged me and even told me about a part-time opening at a small newspaper near my home.

For my interview, the publisher and I sat in a booth at the local coffee shop, while he read over my resume and scrutinized me over the top of his glasses.

"I see here that you studied Cultural Anthropology and French at U.C.L.A."

"Yes, I did." I waited.

"Newspapers report on American culture. And if you know French, you know English grammar. Your background is perfect. You're hired."

I let out the deep breath that I didn't know I'd been holding and had to smile for all the times I'd heard, "You'll never get a job with those majors."

I loved the balance of the days at home with my daughters contrasted with the three days a week working at the newspaper. There, I was a separate person, using my mind and abilities out in the world doing something that I loved—and getting paid for it.

I breathed in the smell of the printing presses when I walked in each morning. In those days, the term "cut and paste" referred to the real process of cutting out stories and ads and pasting them where they needed to go before printing.

I relished the adventure of not knowing what story I'd be assigned and then jumping in and doing it, forming the thoughts, polishing them and then seeing them in print a few days later. It felt so powerful to say "I'm with the newspaper" and gain access to otherwise closed worlds. I'd replaced a woman who was out on sick leave and she was coming back; there were no other writing positions open. But I had tasted the joy of being a writer. I promised myself that someday, I would find a way to be a writer again.

10

At age thirty, I began a new chapter of my life, divorced with two young daughters. Amid all of the challenges of negotiating a new life for us, I also wanted to gain back a sense of myself that I had lost since my marriage. Always, the thrill of speaking French energized me and gave a sparkle to life that I couldn't explain but that I realized, as more time passed, was a cherished gift. It felt like a link back to who I had been, some essential part of myself. So I continued with classes, conversation groups and audiotapes to improve my French skills.

I wasn't able to find a job as a writer, but I had good people skills, so found work in sales and marketing. I still held onto the hope that someday, I could achieve the goal of being a full-time writer.

As I looked at my new life and felt a renewed sense of freedom, it struck me that I had yet to travel to France. My ex-husband had not shared my interest in French and France. In contrast, a few years after my divorce, I began dating a man who thought it would be great fun to travel to France. At thirty-three, I had been longing and waiting since I was fourteen to go; nineteen long years had passed. We booked the trip.

Dad had old-fashioned values and I knew he wouldn't approve of me traveling with someone I was dating. So when

I told him about my trip to France, I was a bit vague and I didn't talk to him much about it. I look back now and wonder why I didn't think about trying to find Gilbert on my trip. But those stories from my childhood were buried far back in my life at that moment, when I was trying to navigate being divorced, working, relationships and a new life.

I'd spent all those years studying French without ever setting foot in the country. It was like I'd been rehearsing to play a part and finally was stepping out onto the stage. As I worked with a tutor to prepare for the trip, I could feel that old magic and excitement coming back into my life. Would the fantasy world I'd created as a teenager and held onto for so long fall apart when I finally fulfilled the dream? I couldn't wait to find out.

The moment I came up from the R.E.R. (*Réseau Express Régional*) train into the street in Paris, all I could do was stare. It felt like I'd stepped into the pictures I had seen all those years ago, with Sharon and Holly in the French I book—the sidewalk *cafés*, crammed with people chatting in French, sipping café out of tiny cups, smoking those long French cigarettes. Waiters scurried about, tiny French cars honked on the busy streets and people rushed past. I stood still, blinked and smiled.

I loved the challenge of speaking French and found us a hotel, for five dollars a night, in the Latin Quarter, near the Sorbonne. The shower down the hall delivered only a spindly stream of hot water, but our room had a tiny balcony with French doors. I was transfixed.

We found our way around the city to see the sights, the Eiffel Tower, the *Arc de Triomphe*, Notre Dame Cathedral, and the tiny chapel of *Sainte-Chapelle*. I did well with the

French, ordering meals and navigating the metro. There was just one major snafu when my friend ordered a "hamburger." When the meal arrived, a piece of bright, red, raw hamburger meat with a fried egg on top decorated the plate.

He, being from the Midwest, was appalled that the meat was raw. The waiter, being French, was appalled that he was appalled. I tried to calm things down as well as I could. We sent it back and it came back *bien cuit*, well done, though the waiter did throw the plate down. Ah well, one rude Parisian waiter wasn't so bad.

We rented a car to tour across France. As we drove through the Rhone Alps, just over the border from Switzerland, we passed Lake Annecy. We only had one afternoon to swim in the sparkling, clear lake, but I vowed that someday, I would come back and spend more time. From Annecy, we took the winding mountain road towards Nice, passing miles and miles of meadows bright with wild flowers.

Late in the day, needing to find a place to stay, we stopped in a tiny village. At the edge of the town square, a rusty "Hotel" sign hung crooked off its hinges. The brown letters were so faded, I could barely make out the sign, *Hotel de la Place*, Hotel on the Square, two stars.

As I entered the lobby to ask about a room, the high ceilings and worn, but elegant furniture made me feel like I'd stepped back in time. I rang the bell on the desk, and an older woman came forward, dusting flour off her hands onto her white apron, her gray hair pulled up in a bun. She seemed a little hesitant, guessing that I was American, but smiled and looked relieved when I spoke to her in French.

Yes, they had a room and it included dinner and breakfast. They grew their own vegetables, raised their own chickens and baked their own tarts, which she had just been doing. *Formidable*. What a find.

Upstairs, in our large, spacious room, right along one wall, stood a modern shower stall; it must have been a recent upgrade. Lace curtains fluttered at the windows, which looked out over the extensive garden and farmyard out back. *La toilette*, the toilet, was across the hall.

That evening, downstairs in the dining room, tall candles flickered on the tables, which were covered with starched, white damask tablecloths and napkins. Our dinner included five simple and tasty courses. A rich "potage" or vegetable soup, fresh green salad, roast chicken and vegetables, a cheese tray and an apple tart with thick cream, all served with a local *Côtes du Rhône* white wine.

The meal had a quality of freshness and flavor both delicious and nourishing. We felt like honored guests as they served us course after course. As I conversed in French, I felt softer and less certain than in English, but there was the connection, the smile of recognition, the moment of bridging what could have been a gap, because we could all understand the same sounds.

In that tiny village, in the hills above Nice, where we were the only Americans, we'd dropped into the old world of France. That one night stands out as such a vibrant memory and confirmed what I already knew—speaking French in the real France was even better than I could have ever imagined.

The next morning, after breakfast in the sunlit dining room, the family bid us goodbye as we set off for the coast. After Nice, we poked our way across France in our tiny rental car, enjoying the little beach towns along the Mediterranean and the open fields of lavender and sunflowers. A few days in Paris at the end, and it was time to go home. But I carried within me the wonder of the trip and was already dreaming of how to return.

Back at home, however, the reality of my life, as a single mother and making my way in the world, meant that thoughts of future visits to France had to go underground again. I listened to French songs, treasured again a French *Vogue* magazine and went to French films, just to have a taste of the language and the culture that so fed my soul.

Why was I fascinated with a place so far away? It was so much more practical to learn and know Spanish, with Mexico just a few miles south of where I lived. But I'd given up long ago trying to solve that mystery. I adored French and now had a real experience of the country. I would find a way to go back.

My daughters and I managed to visit Dad in Hawaii a few times and he came to California, so we saw him about once a year. During the summer of 1986, I had a stretch of six days with no kids and an airline voucher for a free flight. My dad's birthday was July 20th, so I called him and asked if he'd like a very special birthday present—a visit from me! He was thrilled. I hadn't been back to Hawaii in three years and it was such a joy to relax and spend time with Dad.

At the end of my stay, he took me to the airport, and as always, walked me right up to the gate. Dad liked to be early. "Better an hour early than a minute late," he always said, so we had plenty of time before my flight boarded. We found a coffee shop near the gate, with gray Formica tables between brown vinyl covered seats, and sat down.

Dad ordered coffee and his favorite dessert, a piece of apple pie. When his coffee came, he tapped his sugar packet on the table, first one side, then the other, before he put it into his coffee. I'd seen him do that so many times and wasn't sure why he did it, but it made me smile, it was so "Dad."

I drank tea and we chatted about the visit and how great it had been. But there was something I had wanted to say to him for a long time and I sensed that this was the chance.

"Dad, do you remember when I had pneumonia when I was eight and was in the hospital?"

"Of course I do. You were so sick and if it hadn't been for that experimental drug and that new young doctor who was willing to try it, we could have lost you." He frowned and shook his head.

"Well I had an experience there that I always thought was just a dream, but since then, I've read about it a few times. It is called an "out-of-body experience" and is what happens to some people when they are dying and leaving." He nodded, put down his coffee mug and leaned forward.

"That night, you were there, sitting in a metal chair, dozing off, and all of a sudden, I could see you from up above. I was no longer inside my body, but looking down on the whole scene, including me in the bed and you in the chair. Then, I could feel myself floating away through the wall towards a golden glow and I felt so free."

"I was headed towards that glowing light, right through the wall and that is when I woke up to the fact that something must be really wrong—I couldn't move through a wall! I looked back and saw you again, sitting there in the metal chair.

And in that moment, I knew that I was leaving, that I was dying, and that if I let that warm glow pull me out through the wall, I would never come back."

I took his hand across the table.

"I knew that you would be so sad, that it would break your heart. I could feel your love for me and it turned me around and pulled me back into the room. Thank you for being the one who demanded that they do something to save me and for being such a loving presence in my life that I wanted to come back—I couldn't leave."

By that point, we were both crying, holding hands across the gray Formica table in the coffee shop, as travelers bustled all around us, rushing to catch their flights. The waitress hurried by, her rubber-soled shoes squeaking on the linoleum floor, coffee pot poised, ready to lean in to refill Dad's coffee, then glanced at us and kept moving.

I grabbed some paper napkins from the metal dispenser next to the catsup and handed a few to Dad. We wiped our eyes and blew our noses, both unable to speak for a few moments. Thirty years had passed since I'd been lying in that hospital bed, but sitting there in the airport coffee shop, beyond all of the years in between, I could feel how my father's love back then, and now, was real and precious in my life.

It felt so good to thank him for who he'd been and was for me. I had a lot of uncertainty in my life, but knew that I could count on Dad's love. I was so blessed and deeply grateful. We both composed ourselves and sipped some water to calm down.

"Thank you, Diane Mary, for telling me that. I do remember those days in the hospital, and how your life seemed to be hanging by a thread. I'm so grateful that you did come back."

"Me too, Dad."

They called my flight and we gathered up our things, walked to the gate and hugged goodbye. I boarded the plane and could see him standing there, waving, even after everyone else had left. As the plane taxied down the runway, he got smaller and smaller, standing there in his Aloha shirt, till I couldn't see him anymore.

Part IV

1989

11

My dad turned seventy-five in the summer of 1989 and three generations gathered in California for a special weekend. We celebrated his life, told stories and took a group photo with Dad and his wife in the center of all the kids and grandkids. I noticed that Dad seemed thinner and I was concerned, but he said that everything was all right. I so wanted to believe him.

I will always remember the moment when I knew that everything was *not* all right with Dad. It was early 1990, a few months after Dad's big birthday party. I was sitting at my desk, looking out the window overlooking my back yard, the same view I'd looked at so many times before, as we chatted on the phone. He said something about going to the doctor and I immediately picked up on it.

"What's wrong Dad?"

"I'm having some tests," he said.

"What kind of tests?" I could feel a sense of panic as my voice rose in pitch.

"I've been having some weird symptoms and they're trying to figure out what is going on, that's all."

I made him promise that he'd let me know as soon as he found out anything more. He promised. A week later when I called him back, he didn't want to tell me—he was afraid I'd be worried. But I was already worried. I just wanted to know the truth.

I listened in shock as he told me that he had a rare form of cancer called Waldenström's. He was going to go through chemotherapy and they were hopeful that he'd be all right. He had good doctors, he reassured me.

I got off the phone and sat still, staring out the window. My father, who had never taken a sick day in his thirty-five years of working, could not possibly have cancer. His parents had lived to be eighty-five, his grandparents even longer. This could not be happening.

I walked around my house and thought about him over in Hawaii, facing cancer and chemotherapy. I longed to be able to go and see him, but couldn't see how to take time off from my busy life. But what if we didn't have much time left?

I called Dad every few days to see how he was doing. He tried to minimize it, but the chemotherapy was making him really sick and he was having blood transfusions. After a few months of hearing about his suffering, I made a decision.

I would take a leave from my work, move out of my house, put my things into storage and go and spend time with Dad. As soon as I made that choice, I felt a huge sense of relief. It took two months to tie up my life, stuff all my worldly belongings into a storage unit and head to Hawaii. My oldest daughter was in college and my youngest was living with her dad then, so I had the freedom to go.

I spent a month with Dad, helping to take him swimming to Sans Souci beach where we'd gone together through the years. He was weak, but the warm ocean water seemed to relax him. I read him books. I recorded the stories about his childhood, growing up on a farm during the Great Depression.

All those years ago, Dad used to interview us with a wire recorder. Now, I was interviewing him with a tape recorder. He talked again about his time in the war in France, in 1944.

His frail body regained some of its youthful vigor as if somehow tapping into the strong, young man who turned thirty while stationed in Normandy, a lieutenant junior grade who became a full lieutenant by the end of the war. He was tired and nauseated from the chemotherapy and losing his eyesight, but his eyes shone as he talked about his part in the invasion that stopped Hitler's occupation of Europe.

He'd loved his time in the Seabees, building the artificial harbor, the Rhino Ferries, the camp above Omaha Beach, and repairing bridges in nearby towns. I saw then how his job during the war had been to restore and rebuild things, amid the destruction and devastation.

He was reliving the most powerful time in his life and I realized then how much I had never heard before. He'd always been so attentive and supportive in my life, but how much had I paid attention to his? There was so much about my father that I didn't know. He spoke again about Gilbert DesClos. He still said Gilbert's name with a soft G sound, the way the French said it.

"I wonder whatever happened to him," he said, and he became quiet and seemed sad. I patted his fragile hand, wishing there was something I could do. I didn't want to push him and wear him out, so stopped our taping for that day.

When I left at the end of my visit, he seemed stronger and more like his old self. I so hoped that could last. I knew I wanted to return and spend as much time with him as I could so decided to leave Southern California, where the high cost of living meant I couldn't take more time off work. I moved up to the small Northern California mountain town where my sister lived and rented a cozy studio. I was able to work with clients over the phone and, most importantly, Sharon and I were able to help each other cope with the reality of losing our father.

That winter, I couldn't explain why, but I felt drawn to renew my efforts to learn French. I invested in a video series put out by Yale and began again. As I worked with the videos, I was surprised by how much I remembered and how much I understood. I listened and watched in my little studio while cooking, sewing or doing other projects.

I kept in touch with Dad by phone, but could tell that he was struggling so in March, went back to Hawaii for another visit. When I saw him again, it was shocking to see how much he had declined in just eight months. I knew then that Dad would not win his battle with cancer.

I had to accept the painful reality that it was just a matter of time before he would be gone. I couldn't imagine life without him, but I also hated to see him suffering like he was. He'd lost so much weight and was losing his eyesight. He didn't complain, but it was so hard.

We talked about what he believed about life after death. I read him a poem by Mary E. Frye:

> Do not stand at my grave and weep
> I am not there. I do not sleep.
> I am a thousand winds that blow.
> I am the diamond glints on snow.
> I am the sunlight on ripened grain.
> I am the gentle autumn rain.
>
> When you awaken in the morning's hush

I am the swift uplifting rush
Of quiet birds in circled flight.
I am the soft stars that shine at night.

Do not stand at my grave and cry;
I am not there. I did not die.

After I read him the poem, he became very quiet.

"Dad, do you believe that you have a soul that will live on after your body dies?" I asked.

"I'm not sure about that," he responded.

"Well, I believe, like in the poem, that after death, your soul will still be alive, just not in your body."

"Well, that's a comforting thought," he said.

While I was there, I helped to take Dad swimming a few times. It was a challenge to get him in and out of a wheelchair and in and out of a special warm pool. He was so thin, that he got cold really fast, but he seemed to enjoy moving in the water, so it was worth the effort.

I had written a poem for Dad, thanking him for being there for me when I was a child. Now he was living the last days of his life. One day, I was sitting outside with him, watching over him while he walked a few paces back and forth in front of the house.

He stopped and looked at me and I looked up.

"Diane, you know that poem that you wrote?" I nodded.

"That was real nice."

He looked over at me, smiled, then kept shuffling along, holding onto the walls to steady himself as he went. I wiped away a few tears while his back was turned, touched that my poem had meant something to him and that he'd told me.

At the end of my six-week visit, when I said goodbye to Dad, the thought of not seeing him again made me determined to return as soon as I could. I did not want this to be our last goodbye. For the first time, when I left Honolulu,

Dad was not standing at the airport gate and waving. I began to feel the loss of him, piece by piece.

The Ways of the Heart
A poem written for Dad
January 6th, 1991

Time seems to change things, Dad...
I remember...
When I was small, you held my hand
as we crossed the street
you steadied my way and guided me, protected me
while my little legs grew strong and true

We'd stop and rest
I couldn't keep up with your strong long legs

Now I hold your hand as we cross the street
I steady your way
I guide and protect you
Your legs
have grown weak
We stop and rest
you can't keep up with my strong long legs

Thank you, Dad for the gifts you gave me
for showing me love
for teaching me so well
and allowing me to share it back with you

Bodies grow and change
but hearts remember love and
there is no time
in the ways of the heart

12

In the background of my life, always present in my thoughts, I knew my father was fighting for his life. When I talked to him on the phone, his voice had lost its rich timbre; he whispered now. But it was still Dad. He was still there, barely, but still there. I booked my flight to go back.

Summer turned to fall, the days got shorter and the leaves started to turn and float down on the light breeze. This autumn, I knew that I would lose my father. He'd always been there, a light in my sometimes dark life, loving and encouraging. He and my sister Sharon had been my anchors. What would I do without him?

My flight back to Hawaii had been delayed and I arrived late in the evening. But when I walked into the hospital room, Dad was sitting up, eyes open, present and alert. Even though he couldn't see me, he knew I was there the moment I walked in—he looked right where I was in the doorway.

I hugged his frail body and then sat down holding his hands. He couldn't see the tears flowing down my cheeks as we talked. It was so good to see him alive. He asked about the flight, the family. We had a good visit. *He's doing all right,* I thought.

His wife Aileen and I got him settled down for the night. I left and went back to their home, the familiar place I'd visited so many times since Dad had married Aileen, twenty-two years before. The bathroom smelled like Dial soap, with stacks of *Reader's Digest* in the magazine rack and worn towels hanging from the wooden towel racks. I settled into my room and slept, tired from the long journey.

The next morning, I returned to the hospital and when I walked in, he was sleeping. I sat with him and waited for him to wake up so that we could visit. But as the hours passed, he didn't wake up; he'd slipped into a state of semi-consciousness.

As I sat by his bed and watched him, I realized he'd waited for me to arrive so that we could have a real visit— one last conversation. We would never have another conversation like that, like we'd had thousands of times before.

Once or twice that day, he woke up and looked at me for a moment, seemed to be there, then slipped away again. I tried to wake him and to help him to eat when the food came, tried to get him to at least take a sip through a straw of the canned, thick, chocolate drink they brought to feed his skeletal frame. But he didn't have the energy to rally.

The hospital buzzed outside his room, elevator bells chimed, meal and medicine carts rolled down the polished hallways. Once in a while, a nurse came in to check on him for a few moments. They left him alone, as if they couldn't face that he was dying. Except that was just not right.

On the third day, I called in a male nurse and asked him when was the last time they'd changed his bedding, his gown or bathed him? He didn't answer me. And couldn't they please turn him so that he didn't get bedsores? After my insistence, the nurse checked Dad in a perfunctory way. I had to say something.

"He was a pilot, you know. Learned after World War II on the GI bill. He so loved to fly. And an engineer with the Navy, here at Pearl Harbor and in World War II."

The nurse paused, looked up at me and then at Dad. I could see the moment when Dad became a real person for him, not the thin, almost lifeless form lying on the bed. How I wish now we could have taken Dad home; I didn't know then about Hospice.

By the fourth day, I was angry at what felt like their neglect of him; I would take care of him if they wouldn't. I told them I wanted to bathe him, to please bring me all that I needed, dry shampoo, warm water, towels and cloths. And then I wanted a clean gown and sheets for him afterwards.

They brought it all. He was deeply somewhere else by then, only waking up for brief moments and then not knowing where he was, who he was or who I was.

I washed his emaciated body with the warm towels, drying him right off and covering him to make sure that he didn't get cold. Because he was so thin, I could see how huge his frame was, his giant kneecaps, hands and feet, his large head.

As I bathed him, I was reminded of taking care of my two babies when they were tiny. I knew back then, that it mattered that I was gentle and loving, because there was a soul inside that couldn't respond back yet, but that soul knew and felt my love. That day, washing my father's dying body, I knew that he, too, could feel my love, just like my babies had.

I held my hand up to his. I'm not tiny by any measure, but my hand was only half the size of his. He'd always occupied a huge space in my life and now I could see that physically he *was* huge. When they turned him so that I

97

could wash his back, I winced at the bright red bedsore on his lower back.

I washed his hair with dry shampoo, shaved him gently, to make sure I didn't cut his face, then splashed on his favorite aftershave, Aqua Velva, which he'd worn my whole life. It was so Dad, that smell. I brushed his teeth and combed his clean hair, then called them in to change his sheet and gown.

My father had gotten up each day at five forty-five, showered and shaved, splashed on the Aqua Velva, brushed his teeth and was ready for the day. I had never once seen him unclean or unshaven.

He visibly relaxed as he settled back into the fresh sheets, wearing the new gown, his body now clean. Lunch came and again he couldn't wake up to eat. I felt so many emotions—anguish at seeing him like that, sadness, and distress. I held his hand, closed my eyes and prayed.

Dad's uneaten lunch sat on the tray beside him. Shiny red Jell-O, orange-green pureed vegetables, overcooked chicken and another can of the thick chocolate drink. The smell of it made me nauseous. I pushed it away and took his huge hands in mine.

Dad, I said, talking directly to him, psychically. *Dad, I can't stand to see you like this one more minute. You've fought with great courage, but the cancer has won. Please don't hang on for me or for Aileen, trying to protect us from the pain of losing you. The pain of watching you suffer is more difficult. It's okay for you to let go now.*

I'm here till Tuesday. If you let go today, I can call everyone and they'll be able to come. I can organize the memorial services—I can do it all. If you wait, Aileen will have to face it alone and that would be hard for her.

I know that you worry about me, that I'm alone. But I'm strong, Dad. I'll be all right.

You are so precious to me—you taught me how to love by your love. I will miss you and always remember your love and your goodness, but I don't want to remember you like this. You can go now, Dad.

It was early Thursday afternoon. I knew he understood what I'd sent to him with my thoughts. I cried as I sat with him all that afternoon, holding his hand and stroking his face. How mysterious life is, I thought. He'd sat next to my hospital bed, when I was eight, to keep me here. Now I was sitting next to his hospital bed, to help him to let go. The nurses didn't come in. He didn't wake up for dinner.

I left about ten when Aileen came to sleep in the room with him. She'd been doing that for a few nights since he'd been waking up disoriented and frightened, unable to see and not knowing where he was. She'd comfort him and he'd go back to sleep.

The jarring jangle of the old dial telephone woke me up at three in the morning. I had to stumble to another room to answer it, but knew what it was before I picked up the receiver.

"Your dad is gone," Aileen said, her voice soft through the phone line.

"Oh, okay, I'll be right there."

I ran to the bathroom to splash cold water on my face, when the reality hit me. *He's gone. Oh no.* I turned to the towel rack next to the sink to dry my face when I felt a jolt of energy hit me in the chest.

Pow. He was letting me know that he was okay.

Wow, thanks Dad. That helps.

99

Though I couldn't prove to anyone that I'd felt that jolt, I'd felt it. And I knew it was *him*. It lightened the heaviness in my heart.

I made the familiar drive to the hospital, through the deserted streets of Honolulu, parked, ran through the doors, up the elevator to the fifth floor, down the hall past the nurses' station, to the room on the left.

But the bed was empty. They'd already taken him away to the morgue in the basement. They needed the bed for another patient. Just his hearing aid and a few personal items sat on the side table for us to take home.

"Tell me what happened," I said to Aileen. I wanted to know.

"He woke up and was disoriented so I got up to comfort him. I wanted to sing to him, but the only song that came to mind was one that he taught me from his time in England during the war, before France."

"So I started in on *I've got sixpence, jolly, jolly, sixpence, I've got sixpence, to last me all my life...* It seemed to calm him down and I felt better singing it. When I got to the last line, *and we go rolling, rolling home*, he chimed in the last words, *dead drunk*."

"Then he settled down again and I went back to the cot to sleep. It was a while later when the nurse woke me and told me that he had passed."

It was sweet to imagine the scene of Aileen singing to Dad and Dad chiming in the words to a song he'd sung during such a powerful time in his life. I had to smile at the irony, that though my father had never been drunk in his life, his last words had been *dead drunk*.

He had felt the words that I had poured out from my heart the afternoon before. He had let go. I was so glad that he had slipped away in his sleep, with his wife right there beside him.

I kept my word to him and called everyone to come and arranged for two memorial services, one at his church and a military memorial at the Punchbowl Cemetery where his ashes would be interred.

The next challenging task was to write his obituary. I scanned the newspaper to get a sense of what to write. I read one for an eight-year-old girl who had just died, another for a forty-year-old man, then one for a woman in her fifties.

I realized that at seventy-seven, Dad had had a full life. He'd traveled the world, successfully raised four children and four stepchildren, served in two wars and had a busy and active life right up until he got sick. When I finally wrote the words *"Donald Kenneth Johnson, 1914-1991,"* I felt a sense of peace.

Sharon asked to see Dad's body one last time, to be able to say goodbye. Even though this was not what they had planned, Aileen agreed. But that also meant that we had to pick out some clothes for them to dress Dad in. Aileen and I chose his favorite Aloha shirt, a pair of pants, a belt, underwear, socks and shoes. One of their friends offered to drive the clothes over to the funeral home.

"Tell them to be sure to not tuck in his shirt," I said. That one detail was so important, for the last time that we'd see him in those clothes. Otherwise, it just wouldn't be Dad.

"Okay, I will be sure to do that," the friend agreed.

Early Saturday morning, Sharon, Aileen, her youngest son and I went over to the funeral home and sat in the room with Dad's body. He looked like he was sleeping, there in his Aloha shirt that wasn't tucked in. We sat in silence and said goodbye to the physical form of the man who had been such a large and loving presence in our lives. As we left to go back to the house, it began to rain.

101

"In the Hawaiian culture, rain is considered a blessing," Aileen said.

"That's good," I said. The idea of a blessing at that moment felt right.

Later that morning, at the memorial service at Dad's church, the space overflowed with family and friends who came to pay their respects. Dad had been a volunteer with the Coast Guard Auxiliary and a large contingent of his group came in uniform. Dad would have loved that.

We sang "Amazing Grace" and "How Great Thou Art," his mother's favorite hymn, which Dad and I had heard on the car radio, driving around Oahu together when I was eighteen. One of Dad's friends from the church read the poem that I had written for Dad, "The Ways of the Heart." People came back to the house after the service, bringing food and comfort and trying to help us to fill the void.

The following Monday, we gathered again at the Punchbowl Military cemetery. In the ceremony, the solemnity of the taps and the crack of the guns in the twenty-one-gun salute gave a finality to Dad's life and reminded us of his service to his country. They presented a flag to my brother, as the oldest son.

After the ceremony, as we stood around, I looked at the urn of ashes with *Donald Kenneth Johnson* inscribed on it and the tears started to fall. How could my father be in that little box? Right at that moment I felt another jolt of energy and heard Dad's voice, loud and clear, almost shouting in my head, *"Do not stand at my grave and weep, I am not there, I do not sleep."* The words startled me and made me remember the poem I had read to Dad.

Okay, Dad. I forgot for a second there. Thanks for the reminder.

That second sense of him "on the other side" letting me know that he was okay helped to lift the grief and sadness. In the photographs from that day, large white spots appear around my brother as he is holding the flag, just the moment when I started to cry.

Some people say those represent the unseen spirits, their energy caught on the film. I had heard him distinctly, right then, when the photo was taken.

Back at the house, going through Dad's things, Aileen showed me a file from his desk where he kept all my communications with him through the years. For every phone conversation, he jotted down notes. Every letter I wrote was also filed, in order. There was so much love in that file. I held it close to my heart, then added it to my pile of things to take home.

Tuesday morning, I had some time before my flight back to California. I went down to *Sans Souci* beach, that special place I'd discovered at age eighteen and where I'd gone with Dad and our families in the twenty-four years since.

All of my senses felt heightened—the sky seemed bluer, the palm trees greener as they swayed along the shore. The ocean felt cool and refreshing on my skin, as I moved through the water, feeling my strong legs propelling me along.

I'm alive and healthy. Life is such a gift. Thank you, Dad, for showing me that. You're gone now, but I will never forget your love.

I knew that I was still in a state of shock, and that the loss would sink in as time went on. But those moments felt like a gift and a balm as I prepared to leave Hawaii and to begin life without my father.

13

Back home, I retreated to my cozy studio in the chilly fall weather, relishing the simple ritual of lighting the wood stove for warmth and making soups for dinner. Many times I picked up the phone to call Dad before remembering, *Oh that's right. He's gone. I can't talk to him any more.* Being close to my sister and her family and spending time with my daughters helped me to deal with the emptiness.

I also felt soothed by the quiet presence of nature all around me. The huge pines that touched the sky, the stars that twinkled through the tree branches like Christmas lights at night and the subtle changes of the seasons, day by day and week by week.

It was as if nature hit me over the head each time that I walked out of my door and said, *wake up, look around, be present, here, now.* I relaxed into that space and relished the wonder I witnessed each day. After the quiet of a snowy winter, the apple trees at the farm just up the hill burst into fragrant white and pink blossoms, reminding me of the gift of new life that spring represents.

I had not been back to France since that first trip in 1982, but could feel the mysterious pull and the longing to go again. For two years after my dad's death, I watched my French videos, soaking my brain with the melodious sounds and learning new words and phrases. I also still held onto the hope of finding a way to become a writer again.

In 1993, I took a class at the community college on how to be a successful freelance writer and the teacher kept emphasizing the importance of writing about what we were passionate about. When I realized that the 50th anniversary of D-Day was coming up the following June, I decided to write an essay telling how growing up with Dad's stories about the war and France had influenced my life.

And what if I could somehow journey back to Normandy, to remember and to honor Dad? With both of my daughters in college, I could arrange the time to go. When a friend offered me his air miles to make the journey, I knew it was the chance I'd been waiting for. I booked my flight.

A few weeks later, after taking the train from Paris to the shiny, modern train station in Rennes, I sat alone on a bench waiting for my connection to Bayeux. A kind man asked me where I was headed and when I showed him my ticket, he pointed out a train a few tracks over—I was sitting in the wrong place. I ran and jumped on the vintage, red train just at the last moment before the conductor blew the whistle.

We chugged along through the Normandy countryside, passing apple trees laden with bright red fruit and hefty black and white cows munching the fall grass. I left my empty compartment to stand in the aisle and lowered the large metal window to let in the fresh October air.

I was forty-four years old. I had been studying French for thirty years, with just one trip to France. But on this trip, my second, I was fulfilling my dream of traveling alone on the train, finding my way, speaking the luscious sounds to buy baguettes, cheese and fruit and to find a hotel.

I felt the significance of traveling back to the Normandy coast where my father had spent over four months during the war and excited to write an essay in his honor for the 50th anniversary of the D-Day invasion. I hugged myself in a glow of happiness and satisfaction as I stood at the window, felt the cool breeze and watched the landscape change as the train chugged and hooted along its way west.

At the family-run, one-star hotel in the village of Bayeux, where I'd reserved a room, the young woman at reception welcomed me warmly. When I mentioned that I was researching an article about the D-Day invasion in honor of my father, she told me that a group of English World War II Veterans were also staying in the hotel and encouraged me to meet them that evening when they gathered.

I carried my bag up the narrow wooden stairs to my third-floor room, which looked out over rooftops and across to the cathedral. The tiny room consisted of a double bed, covered by a worn but clean comforter, an antique dresser with a white embroidered doily on top and a sink, with clean white towels. The *toilette* and shower were down the hall. *Perfect.*

That afternoon I wandered and explored the town, visiting the cathedral and the famous Bayeux tapestry. The quaint village had escaped extensive bombing during the war and the Norman buildings and winding streets retained their old-world charm.

The next day, I was scheduled to take an intense, all-day tour of the D-Day Invasion beaches, so I enjoyed my leisure time. At lunch, I sat in the sun at an outdoor café near a rushing creek and enjoyed a salad and a glass of white wine, relishing the joy of living in French in this corner of France.

That evening, as I came into the hotel again after dinner, the receptionist told me that the English Veterans, who were gathered in a room off the lobby, wanted me to join them. When I walked into the room, about thirty elderly men sat at tables, chatting. They were in their late sixties and seventies, many of them wearing their brown, belted uniforms from the war, some covered in medals.

Their caps, jaunty wool berets, and a few officer-style hats, sat on the tables. Their hair was white and their faces wrinkled, but they became animated, their eyes twinkling, as they laughed and kidded each other and told stories of their time together in France all those years before.

They were enjoying their dessert course, an apple tart, and insisted on ordering one for me. Large carafes of wine and a few bottles of whisky and Calvados circulated among the tables. They welcomed me like a long-lost daughter and I felt honored to be included in their gathering. As I told them about Dad's part in the war, they listened and nodded their heads.

One very frail man stood up to speak, wobbling as he leaned on his cane, his voice coming out just above a whisper. A younger soldier jumped up to stand by his side, to help him if needed. The older man had a lot of medals on his uniform and everyone leaned forward to listen to his words with respect. They were remembering the glory that they had shared in being a part of such a major event in history.

As the evening went on, when they mentioned members of their group who had died, either in the invasion or since, many of them wiped away tears. Their frailness and sweetness reminded me so much of my dad that I also became teary. Had Dad's battalion gotten together like this too, I wondered? If so, he had never talked about it. They gave me hugs, pats and many hand squeezes before I said goodnight, wishing me well with the tour and with my story.

The next day, I wiped away tears as I stood on the cliffs above Omaha Beach, where my father had stood almost fifty years earlier, before I was born. The all-day tour taught me so much about the invasion that turned the tide of World War II and began the defeat of Adolf Hitler. Knowing the whole story also created a new context or backdrop for my father's stories.

Now I was there after my father's death, retracing his steps and remembering him, his stories and his love. It all felt poignant and important, as if something inside of me was saying, *pay attention now, slow down and listen.*

Being there, where it had all happened, also made me think about Gilbert DesClos. As a child, I'd been fascinated with the idea that I could have had a French brother and also always felt the incompleteness of the story, how it was all left hanging. What had happened to him?

As a stared out over the English Channel, my thoughts kept returning to Gilbert. He must be real because I now knew that all the other stories were real. What if he had been waiting somehow, for some word from Dad or for Dad to come back? By now, it had been fifty years. The boy, now a man, might not even remember what happened. And how on earth could I ever find him when I was not even sure how to spell his last name?

But then again, what if I could find him?

14

On June 6th, 1994, the 50th anniversary of the invasion, my essay, "Touching the Heart of D-Day" appeared in several newspapers. It described my journey back to Normandy and how Dad's stories about his time in France had colored my childhood, especially the one about his relationship with Gilbert DesClos. I was thrilled to have sold a freelance essay about a topic that meant so much to me and to restart my writing career.

The TV was full of specials about World War II, with powerful images of young soldiers landing on the beaches, laden down with packs and guns, running and dodging the rat-a-tat of German bullets. I watched all the specials, adding to the knowledge I'd gained on my tour the previous fall.

Thousands of Veterans, now in their late sixties and seventies, were traveling back to France, many of them for the first time since the war, to remember and to honor their fellow soldiers who had died and never returned home. The touching ceremonies at the American cemetery above Omaha Beach felt especially moving, reminding me of my powerful visit. I was excited to be returning to France in a few weeks with my daughter and taking part in the 50th anniversary celebrations that continued throughout the month of June.

When my youngest daughter Heather was fourteen and started studying French, we made a deal that if she continued with her studies of the language, then, when she was nineteen, we'd travel to France together for a month.

I thought Heather might change her mind between fourteen and nineteen, and want to travel with her friends—the backpack, Eurail pass, youth-hostel trip. But at nineteen, she still wanted to take the trip with me.

Because of my success with the D-Day essay, I set up other articles to write, about traveling with Heather and about French seawater therapy spas, which I'd read were healing and wonderful. When Heather was home on breaks from college, we'd watch French videos together, knowing we were practicing for our upcoming journey in June.

During the busy weeks before the trip, something told me to send a copy of my D-Day article to the French Consulate in San Francisco. They had someone there called a press attaché who might be interested. So I followed that hunch, and wrote a quick note attached to the article, saying I would be in France for the ongoing 50th anniversary celebrations.

A few days later, the press attaché from the Consulate called and invited me to meet with her before I left for France. At the Consulate, I felt as though I had dropped into a tiny island of France and relished hearing French spoken all around me.

The press attaché welcomed me into her elegant office and thanked me for the heartfelt article. She nodded and smiled as we chatted about my upcoming trip with my daughter. Then she leaned forward and spoke with great intensity.

"Madame Covington, while you are in Normandy, you must try to find the orphan Gilbert DesClos."

I paused, touched by her interest in the story, but not sure how I could do what she asked. I'd thought about looking for Gilbert on this trip; I'd had the conversation in my head, over and over: Was it possible? How would I look for him? Could I find him and would he even remember?

"Yes, I would like to try to find him. But I don't know how to even begin," I replied. "And it's been fifty years!"

"I know, but you don't understand. The French don't move around like *'les Américains'*. He will still be right there, in Normandy," she insisted.

"Here is what you do. You place a *petite annonce*, a little ad in the newspaper in Normandy. It's called *Ouest France*."

She turned to the side of her desk and looked up the address and phone number of the newspaper on her Minitel computer-like device, wrote it on a slip of paper and handed it to me. I put it into my wallet where I knew I wouldn't lose it. As I stood up to leave, she took my hand and held it as she spoke.

"Madame Covington, promise me you will try to find the orphan Gilbert. Promise me you will place the ad."

I paused and looked back at her, quieting my busy mind, full of pre-trip preparations, for just that moment. She had given me hope that finding my father's orphan could be possible.

"I promise," I said.

I was excited about the chance that I might find Gilbert DesClos. And yet, it still seemed like a remote possibility and I assumed that it would take months or years to find Gilbert, if at all. I was mainly focused on the trip ahead with Heather, thrilled that I was taking her to France when she was nineteen, the age when I had so wanted to go.

I'd worked for months creating a full itinerary for us, from Normandy to Nice and back again. Just before our trip, I stayed up late one night, typing out our itinerary with all the phone numbers for my sister. Something told me to include the fax numbers listed at each place, even though neither Sharon nor I had a fax. I couldn't have explained why to anyone, but I felt compelled to put those numbers in there.

I listed every appointment I had, even places we were just stopping for lunch, where I had a meeting with a local person to gather information for one of my articles. I couldn't think why Sharon might need to try and reach us, but I put all those details on the itinerary.

I handed the neatly typed pages over to Sharon just before I left, in a red file folder labeled in bold black letters: "Diane and Heather's itinerary for France trip, 1994." Sharon put it on the counter next to her phone in her kitchen. In her busy life as the mother of three, she would be able to find it there.

Heather and I flew to Paris and spent a few days discovering the "City of Light" together. We toured the Louvre, sipped cafés in sidewalk bistros, visited Notre Dame cathedral, strolled along the Seine and sampled the best vanilla ice cream in the world.

From Paris, we picked up our rental car and headed west to Normandy. As we drove into the region, huge banners hung over the roads for the Fiftieth Anniversary of D-Day celebrations. *Bienvenue les Américains, Bienvenue nos Libérateurs.* Welcome Americans, Welcome Our Liberators. The banners featured a photo of two smiling French children, a boy and a girl, held by two American soldiers.

"That could have been Dad and Gilbert," I told Heather as we encountered the banners everywhere. I looked forward to taking part in some of the anniversary celebrations.

For my article on French spas, we settled into a seaside spa for a few days of algae wraps, seawater baths, massages and soaks in warm seawater pools. Heather got over some of her post-exams fatigue and we both recovered from jet lag as we relaxed and unwound.

Our last day in Normandy, Heather and I drove to the American cemetery above Omaha Beach, which was busy with returning soldiers and their families. We overheard a conversation with a guide who was helping an elderly American woman find the grave of her husband, who had died in the invasion; we both felt the power and poignancy of that moment.

Heather and I walked along the cliff, which looked down upon Omaha Beach and past the continuous rows of white crosses. Both of us felt the sobering reality that if my father's name had been on one of those crosses, we wouldn't be standing there together.

We then drove to the city of Caen for a ceremony honoring returning soldiers and their families. Heather and I were the only women in the town hall as I lined up, as the daughter of a veteran, with the soldiers or their sons.

The elderly mayor stood in front of each one of us, pinned on a medal and, with tears in his eyes, recited a short speech of gratitude, first in French and then in heavily accented English. I couldn't stop the tears from falling, looking at the old soldiers, remembering Dad and being so touched by the sincere gratitude of the mayor.

After the ceremony, we all stood, shy and awkward, sipping champagne and munching cookies.

Heather had not slept well the night before, still getting used to the time difference and was anxious to leave. Between the cemetery and the ceremony, it had been a moving and emotional day. I thanked the mayor, and Heather and I walked back to our tiny rental car. This was my moment to find the newspaper office and to place the ad to try to find Gilbert DesClos.

"Just put the seat back and rest, listen to your music and I'll dash down the street and place this ad," I said. I had noticed when we parked that we were on the same street as the newspaper *Ouest France*.

Heather seemed so tired and restless that there was a moment when I thought that maybe I shouldn't take the time. But then I remembered the end of my meeting with the press attaché in San Francisco and her insistence that I might be able to find Gilbert.

"I'll hurry. I have to try," I said. "I promised. And this is my chance to try to complete something important for my dad that he was unable to do before he died, to try to find his orphan Gilbert."

"Okay," she said. She put the seat back and punched in the cassette of her favorite music that she had recorded for the trip. I ran down the street searching for the newspaper's address, then spotted the sign, *Ouest France*. After bounding up the steps two at a time, I burst into the front door, startling the young receptionist seated there.

"Excuse me, I would like to place a *petite annonce* in the newspaper," I said, trying to catch my breath.

"It concerns the war and the anniversary. I'm looking for someone," I added.

Something changed in her face when I said those last words, "*Je cherche quelqu'un,*" I'm looking for someone. She paused, then got up from her desk.

"Yes Madame, of course. One moment, if you please." When she returned, she smiled and beckoned for me to follow her.

"Please come this way."

The receptionist ushered me into the office of Monsieur Champion, who stood to welcome me and motioned to a chair. The story tumbled out—of how I was hoping to find the orphan my father tried to adopt fifty years earlier. Monsieur Champion was visibly moved by the tale and reassured me that the newspaper was happy to place the ad at no cost, to appear the following day.

I told him that I was leaving to begin a tour of France with my daughter and because I believed it might take months or even years to find Gilbert, if I found him at all, I gave my home address in California for the ad. I thanked him and excused myself to hurry back to Heather.

I felt relieved that I had fulfilled my promise to the press attaché but sure that my chances of finding my father's orphan were slim at best—I wasn't even sure how to spell his last name. I lived over five hundred miles from the small town where I grew up, so no one could find me from a newspaper ad there. Yet maybe the press attaché was right. Maybe he still was in Normandy. It was so worth the try and placing the ad was the best chance I had. And they had been so kind to me at the newspaper.

Heather and I were heading south and east toward more French spas and other delightful adventures in our carefully planned itinerary. Thinking of the trip ahead and doubting that I could find or hear from Gilbert DesClos soon, if at all, I steered our rental car through the winding streets of Caen and left Normandy behind in the rear-view mirror.

The next morning, Heather and I awoke in a luxurious room in the *Relais De Margaux*, near Bordeaux. We spent the day lounging by the pool, reading and then jogging down narrow country lanes lined with vineyards bulging with dark purple grapes. In the evening, we drove two kilometers for dinner at the one quite wonderful restaurant in the nearby village.

15

That same morning, back in Normandy, just a few miles from Caen, Gilbert DesClos was preparing his early morning cup of strong coffee when the phone rang. His wife Huguette had just left for work and this was his time to sit in his chair, enjoy his coffee and the morning paper.

The jangling of the phone in the hall startled him. Who could be calling this early? Had his wife's car broken down? Or was it his daughter, Cathy? Was one of his grandsons sick?

As he lifted the receiver, he heard his neighbor Pierre shouting: "Gilbert, Gilbert, hurry, you must open the paper. There is a *petite annonce*. Someone is looking for you."

Gilbert thanked him, hung up the phone, grabbed the paper and searched for the ad. Then he saw it.

"The daughter of Lt. Donald K. Johnson looks for Gilbert DesClos, Du Clos, not sure of the spelling of the last name. During the war, this Naval officer took Gilbert under his wing, and now Johnson's daughter would like to find him. Please write to Diane Covington, P.O. Box 1122, Nevada City, California."

Gilbert slumped down into his chair, put his face into his hands and wept. Could this be possible? After fifty years, could he finally be hearing from his beloved Lieutenant Johnson?

Gilbert had told his wife, his daughter and his grandsons the stories of those precious months during the war when the kind naval officer took him through the food line every day and even tried to adopt him and take him home to America.

And most of all, Gilbert thought, as the memories flooded back to him, he had learned from Lieutenant Johnson what it meant to be *loved.*

Gilbert had told his family that one day, his American family would come and find him. He wasn't sure if they believed his words, but it seemed like they wanted him to have his story about the loving man who had been the only father he had ever known. After all these years, Gilbert had even wondered at times if *he* had imagined his Lieutenant Johnson, a fantasy father, to help relieve the lonely pain of never being adopted.

For every major anniversary celebration of the D-Day invasion, when American soldiers returned to Normandy, Gilbert waited and hoped. But nothing, year after year. Until now. He dried his tears and read the ad again.

Before he had time to call his wife, four more friends called to make sure he had seen the newspaper. When he finally did reach his wife Huguette, and told her the news, she cried too. She found a copy of the newspaper and called him back, excited to share his joy.

He took a few sips of the now almost cold coffee and calmed himself. His wife told him to call the newspaper office and see if they had any more information about the daughter. Yes, he would do that. He walked to the phone in the hall and, with shaking hands, dialed the number of the office of *Ouest France* and was put through to Monsieur Champion.

Monsieur Champion was thrilled to realize that the American woman's search for her father's French orphan had been fulfilled so quickly. Sadly, he had to tell Gilbert that she had left the area to begin a tour of France. Gilbert felt stunned that he had come so close to reconnecting with his American family and somehow had missed them. He called his wife Huguette back and told her the news.

"Don't worry, we'll write a letter tonight and send it to California. Maybe there's a way that she will find out before she leaves France. Monsieur Champion did say she was planning on staying for a month, remember?"

Gilbert agreed and hung up the phone. But he felt anxious, emotional and unsettled. So many feelings that he had buried for so long began to surface. He sat down in his chair and leaned back. Images played like movies in his mind, scenes he had relived over and over, so full of comfort and love in the barren landscape of his childhood.

Now he knew that they were real. He had not imagined his Lieutenant Johnson who had loved him. He closed his eyes and let the tears flow.

JUNE 6TH, 1944

Before dawn, Gilbert, age seven, had been awakened by his caretaker, Madame Bisson, and hurried to hide in the root cellar in the garden. Madame Bisson, her granddaughter Georgette, Gilbert's friend and playmate, and Gilbert huddled together, listening to the roar of planes overhead, the blasts of gunfire and feeling the ground shake with the explosion of bombs.

Madame Bisson whispered that this could be the long-awaited invasion they had all prayed for. Friends in the French Underground had said that the English and Americans were going to be landing to fight the Germans.

After four years of German occupation, were their prayers finally to be answered?

They stayed in the cellar until late morning. When Madame Bisson peered out, she was startled to see an American paratrooper lying in the dirt among the neatly planted rows of lettuces. She crept out to look and discovered sadly that the young man was unmoving. She hustled the children back into the house and waited for the rest of the day and evening. Gunfire rang out and soldiers ran down the narrow lane beside the house, making it too dangerous to go out.

The next morning, the young man in the garden still had not moved and Madame Bisson knew the worst; he had died fighting for their freedom. A neighbor came by and they all worked together to dig a grave at the back of the garden, draping the soldier in his parachute and laying him gently into the ground. Even Gilbert helped with his own small shovel, feeling the solemnity of the occasion.

Madame Bisson kept the children indoors for almost two weeks, until it seemed as if the fighting had moved farther inland and things had quieted down. Gilbert sat by the window, waiting for the day when he and Georgette would be free again to play and explore outside, hiding in the tall grass and running along the cliffs above the beach below.

He could see from the front window that a camp was springing up just below his house. He ached to get closer and watch. Finally, the day came when Madame Bisson gave him permission to go outside, as long as he didn't go far.

At first light, Gilbert ran to the farthest edge of the yard and sat in the tall grass. He shivered in the brisk sea air as he watched the field below. Such commotion and so many things moving about—Jeeps, trucks, and men carrying huge bags with writing on them. He could smell food cooking nearby from a big tent and breathed in the delicious smells. He put his hand on his thin stomach to stop it from growling.

He ventured down a little closer to where he could see a tall man who held a clipboard and seemed to be in charge. Gilbert noticed how the men in the white caps saluted the other man. Gilbert crept down a little further to watch, then didn't move as the hours passed and the morning turned into mid-day.

Gilbert woke up in his chair and shook his head. He must have dozed off and been dreaming. Then he spotted the open newspaper on the table beside him and remembered. Oh yes, the ad, the daughter, of course. He read it again. It didn't matter that he had already read it dozens of times. He would read it again and again, letting it sink into his brain and his senses. He had waited so long.

Huguette was coming home early from work to help him to write the letter. Then they would take it to the post office and send it to America, to California. Just perhaps it could reach there in time for someone to contact the daughter while she was still in France. They had to try. Every minute seemed to matter.

His daughter Cathy called from work to express her excitement. The whole village knew the story now, it seemed. They were all so happy for Gilbert. Such good news.

Now, if he could just find the daughter.

Many miles south, along the road from Bordeaux to Auch, the next stop on our tour, Heather and I were lost. The French road signs didn't match the map. Added to that, at the roundabout where the road, without warning, became a circle and the destinations spread out like the rays of the sun, the names of those towns also didn't match the map.

Heather wiggled and squirmed in our tiny car, groaning as she attempted to stretch her right leg out of the window.

"How much farther till we get there?"

I was trying to read the map and road signs while staying clear of the other cars on the narrow lane. Meanwhile, Heather's music blared from the tape player.

"Heather, could you please turn the music down? I can't think when it is so loud!" She complied but shot me an exasperated look.

We had been driving for hours but seemed to be only halfway to our destination. When I had planned this trip, everyone told me France was the size of Texas. I'd never been to Texas, but it was beginning to dawn on me that it was a lot bigger than I had realized. But what to do? I'd already arranged all of our hotels and we had to drive.

Hours later, we arrived, hot and tired at the Hotel de France, in Auch. We were to dine on succulent duck breast and delectable desserts. The Tour de France bicycle race was passing by, just a few kilometers away, so we got caught up in that excitement.

We had no idea of the drama that was unfolding with Gilbert DesClos.

That afternoon, Huguette came home early as promised, giving her husband a long hug.

"*Enfin, c'est arrivé.*" Finally, it has happened.

She had always wanted to believe Gilbert's stories about the kind officer who tried to adopt him during the war. At times she even wondered if it was all a fantasy, but what harm would that be, she thought. What lonely child wouldn't want to imagine a person like he had described his lieutenant to be?

But now, it was real. And best of all, for Gilbert, a possible reunion with the American family that he almost became a part of, who were trying to find him.

They sat down at the dining table and got out some fine white paper that Huguette reserved for her letters. Together, they composed a three-page emotional letter to the daughter, remembering her father, his love and the time he and Gilbert shared in 1944.

The letter ended with their address, phone, and the hope that this reached her in time for a reunion while she was still in France. They sealed it and walked hand-in-hand to *La Poste*, a few blocks up in the village, and sent it to America, to California, the fastest way possible.

God speed, thought Huguette as the postmistress took the letter. *May it bring back good news to Gilbert. And soon.*

On our journey, Heather and I found some relief from the long drives by stopping at parks and rest stops to take breaks. With her nineteen-year-old energy and exuberance, she liked to jog around the parks and I kept up as best as I could. In one, we found a giant teeter-totter and laughed and shrieked, hair flying as we sailed through the air, up and down, both feeling about ten years old.

We had looked forward to this trip for years and I so wanted it to turn out well. I kept trying to figure out a solution to the long drives. After Nice, we faced at least a twelve-hour drive across France to our last destination before Paris, the resort towns of Pornichet and La Baule along the Atlantic coast. And with our penchant for getting lost, it would take us longer. We were both dreading all those hours in the car, so I hatched a plan.

I talked Hertz into allowing us to leave our car in Nice, fly to Nantes, near our destination, and pick up another car there. After all, we would be putting so many fewer miles on the car! It took quite a few phone calls but, to our good fortune, a friendly customer service representative agreed to my plan.

It was a thrill to soar over France, covering in just over an hour the distance that we would have struggled across in the heat in our car. In Nantes, we drove the short drive to our last stop, the towns of Pornichet and La Baule, along the Côte d'Amour, where the wide, sandy beaches reminded us of California.

I had arranged for us to rent a small, furnished apartment where we could settle in for a week. We'd been on the move for two weeks since we left Normandy and it felt good to stop and relax. The area had more of the seawater therapy spas, for my articles.

We'd been in hotels, some large and luxurious and some quaint, with rooms no bigger than the bed, and they'd all been charming. In contrast, now we had our own kitchen, so we could go to the open markets and buy fresh fruits, vegetables and cheese, to the *boulangerie* for fresh *baguettes* and *pain au chocolat*, then go on a picnic or come home to our little place to fix meals, just like the locals.

We were near the end of our trip, so both Heather and I were feeling confident in the language and enjoying the challenges of negotiating day-to-day life in French. It had been so special to have this time together discovering France.

16

My sister Sharon lived a busy life, with a husband and three active children. She fixed healthy meals and drove the kids to all their activities, coming and going in an old red Jeep, with fake wood paneling on the side. When I asked her to pick up my mail at my post office box, she agreed to go whenever she could.

On one hectic day, she ran into the post office and gathered the mail. It had been a while, so the box overflowed with letters. One large envelope stood out from the rest, she noticed, as she headed back to the car. She tended to run late and this particular afternoon, was hurrying to get her son home for a violin lesson.

She stashed the mail in the front passenger seat, next to a bag of groceries. Once home, the mail got deposited at the end of the kitchen counter, on top of the red folder labeled "Diane and Heather's Itinerary."

At eight o'clock, after dinner and dishes, she had a moment to stand at the kitchen counter and take a breath. Her eyes caught the large brown envelope in the stack of mail again. *Maybe I should look at that*, she thought. But then the phone rang and the thought was lost again in the conversation.

It was after nine when, as she straightened up the counter just before turning off the kitchen light, she saw the corner of the large envelope again in the pile of mail. The stamp looked foreign—was it *French*? She shifted the pile so that she could get a better look.

It *was* a French stamp and the envelope said *par avion*, airmail. She fished the envelope out of the stack and noticed the neat, feminine handwriting, then read the return address in the upper left-hand corner, *Gilbert DesClos*.

"Oh my God," she said out loud. "Oh my God," she repeated, as she ripped open the envelope, pulled out the letter and started reading the French.

It was *him*. It was the orphan Dad had tried to adopt. Diane had found him. She'd found him. Tears streamed down her cheeks as she read through the letter.

He is real. He is alive. He remembers Dad. Diane said that she was going to try to find him, but I didn't think that she would. I mean, after fifty years?

She remembered how their Dad had talked about Gilbert during her last visit, the summer before he died. The boy had meant a lot to him. She continued to read the letter, feeling the deep emotions behind the words as she made out more of them with her rusty French.

This is amazing. But then she paused. Except that Diane doesn't know about this letter and she's still there. Oh, I hope it is not too late to get this to her somehow. I have to try to let her know. Sharon opened up the folder with the itinerary and checked the calendar on the wall above her, to match up all the dates and places. There was one phone number and fax number for a meeting and luncheon for the next day, the last contact listed.

With the nine-hour time difference, if she could fax the letter, it would get there in time. But who had a fax? A good friend Sarah and her husband had one, so she called them, apologizing for the late hour, told them the story and asked if she could come over and fax the letter back to France.

That would get the fax there in the morning, just in time for Diane to get it when she went to the meeting and luncheon. Sarah and her husband were glad to try to help, so Sharon headed over to their house. It was after eleven before they got the fax to go through, after a few failed tries and figuring out the long-distance country codes. They drank some cognac to celebrate and shared a toast that the letter would find her in time.

But what if she had changed her plans? They all agreed to not think about that, but to imagine the letter somehow getting into Diane's hands, creating a reunion between Diane and Gilbert.

It was all up to fate at this point.

When the tourist office in Pornichet, France, opened at nine the next morning, a stack of faxes waited to be sorted. The young woman whose job it was to get them to the right staff member noticed that a three-page personal letter to a Ms. Covington had been the last fax to come in. From her brief glance, she also saw that the letter seemed very emotional and personal.

Confused by this, she asked her older co-worker what to do. They figured out that the letter was addressed to the American writer who was meeting with their director for a tour and lunch. They'd have to give her the letter if she came back after lunch.

"We need to make sure that she gets this," the young woman said, looking at the letter. "It seems that she has found someone she was looking for—something about her father, a boy and the war."

"All right then, let's make sure someone is here to give it to her if she comes back."

Gilbert and Huguette had been anxious and waiting since the day they mailed the letter to California. They no longer discussed it out loud, but both had the same recurring thoughts. Would the daughter find out about the letter in time? If not, when would she come back to France? It could be years.

But they didn't talk about that. They talked about the fact that the month wasn't over yet, that there was still hope. Every time the phone rang, they jumped. But the days and weeks passed and she didn't call.

Heather and I had loved our time in Pornichet and La Baule, a quiet time of swimming at the beach, walking, and exploring the towns and area. We visited two local spas, our favorite French discovery—to be painted again with hot algae and wrapped up to rest, then rinsed off, feeling cleansed and revived.

The trip had turned out better than we could have imagined and we were relaxed and laughing as we packed up and loaded the car. I had one more meeting that morning and our plan was to stop and stay somewhere on the drive back to Paris. Then, after one last night in Paris, we would fly back to California early the following morning.

I noticed that the date was July 20th, my dad's birthday. He would have been eighty that day. I held him in my thoughts as we went about our morning.

Heather came along with me on my tour with the director of the tourist office. We enjoyed lunch at an outdoor café, then walked back to her office to say goodbye. As we turned to leave, a shy young woman came around from the back, a letter in her hand.

"Madame Covington, you have a fax."

I looked at the young woman, puzzled. *Who even knew where I was?* By then, I'd forgotten all about the itinerary in the red folder on Sharon's kitchen counter. That seemed so long ago, before we had even started our journey.

She handed me the letter. When I glanced at the return address in the top left hand corner, I stopped and said in English, "Oh my God," then started to cry. Everyone waited while I tried to compose myself, but as I kept reading, the tears continued to fall. I felt both disbelief and awe that I could be reading a letter written by Gilbert DesClos.

"*Qu'est-ce-que c'est?*" What is it? the manager whispered.

I told her briefly how I'd placed the ad to try to find my father's French orphan and that this was a letter from him, the first communication in fifty years. She took a quick breath in and took charge.

"Madame Covington, you must come right now and call him. Do not wait another minute," she said, taking my arm and leading me into the back office. Everyone stood and watched as the story spread in whispered tones.

I sat down at her desk and picked up the phone with a shaking hand. What would I say? How would I begin? It doesn't matter, I thought. Just call. I dialed the number and heard it ringing. Then a man answered.

"*Allo?*" I took a breath and began.

"*Gilbert? C'est Diane, ici, Diane Covington, la fille de Donald.*" Gilbert? It's Diane here. Diane Covington, the daughter of Donald.

I fought back the emotions that tightened my throat and heard him take a sharp breath in—he was crying too. We both stammered through the conversation. We sorted out that yes, I was still in France. He wanted to know if we could meet. I turned to Heather. She nodded.

Gilbert invited us to come back to Normandy to meet them and to spend the night. I agreed and took down the name of a café in Caen where we could rendez-vous later that afternoon.

I set down the phone and stared, still stunned. What if I hadn't come back to the office after lunch? What if we'd changed our plans? How had Sharon managed to fax me this letter? But she *had* managed to fax the letter and we *hadn't* changed our plans.

I sighed and smiled at all the office staff who waited, talking quietly, some of them wiping away tears. As I said goodbye to them and thanked the tourist office director, she gripped my hand hard.

"*Bonne chance avec la réunion.*" Good luck with the reunion.

"*Merci.*"

Outside in the bright midday sun, I tried to remember where I'd parked the car. The world had shifted since earlier that morning. I'd found Gilbert. I still couldn't believe it. We were on our way to meet him. And on Dad's eightieth birthday. *Oh Dad, if only you could have been here for this.*

Heather and I found our car and headed for the main road for the three-hour drive back to Normandy. I appreciated Heather's willingness for the detour, knowing it added extra hours of driving.

"Of course, Mom. You have to go. We have to do this for Grandpa," she said, when I thanked her.

As we drove along, I worried a bit. What if they were not nice people? That would be one thing if I was alone, but I was taking Heather there. Yet the letter was so beautifully written, and sweet. The way he described his memories of Dad was so touching. They must be good people. And talking to him on the phone, it felt right to go. I just had to trust.

We followed the signs back to Caen and Heather helped me with the map. We'd come so far since the beginning of the trip, now working together as a team. She'd taught me all the words to her favorite songs on her tape and I'd taught her some old Frank Sinatra standards from my childhood—"All The Way" and "When I Fall in Love." We sang together, windows down, our voices carried on the breezes, out over the fields of sunflowers and grain.

We arrived in Caen a few minutes early and found the café where we were to meet Gilbert. As we sat and waited, I fidgeted in my metal café chair, searching the faces of people passing by. Could it really be possible that I was waiting to meet Gilbert DesClos, the boy from my childhood stories? And how would I know him?

All around us, the French took long puffs on their *Gauloises* cigarettes. They were all having an ordinary day, a coffee at four o'clock, or a glass of wine, before heading home to their normal life. But my life did not feel normal at all; it felt surreal, like I'd shifted back in time to the yellow Formica table with my father and his stories of France.

Except that now I was *in* the story too, about to meet his special orphan. And it wasn't the past, but the present. I was no longer a child and neither was Gilbert. My mind whirled.

I had never smoked, but right then, wished I could grab a cigarette and light up, just to have something to do with my hands. We waited. Then a trim, well-dressed man walked up to us, smiled and said my name, "*Diane*," which he pronounced "*Deeahhne*," and held out his hand.

133

"*Gilbert,*" he said simply, then gave me four kisses, the warm greeting of Normandy, reserved for special family and friends. His wife Huguette, stood right behind him, smiling, then greeted both Heather and me the same way.

Gilbert, Huguette and I stood, awkward and crying, trying to compose ourselves in the crowded café. Huguette handed out tissues. I don't remember the first words we said to each other. I do remember that when I looked into Gilbert's eyes, I saw the same soft expression of kindness that Dad always had; Gilbert, though not as tall as Dad, actually resembled him somehow.

But he wasn't related to Dad. What was I thinking? Yet from that first moment, Gilbert felt like family. He told me that he knew who I was because I looked so much like my dad. After fifty years, he remembered what my dad had looked like, enough to recognize me.

We decided to go back to their home, where we could talk more easily, and discussed where to meet on the street so that Heather and I could follow behind their car. I kept realizing I was talking to Gilbert DesClos so normally, discussing directions.

This was real. Gilbert was real. I had found him.

17

Gilbert and Huguette lived in Colombelles, a small village a short drive from Caen. Their home, a sturdy stone building over two hundred years old, had been in Huguette's family for generations; Huguette had been born there.

Just inside the entrance hall, across from where coats, boots and umbrellas were organized, the telephone sat on a small table. Behind the hall, a tiny kitchen connected to the garden by way of a laundry room, where Huguette kept finches in a cage just inside the door to the garden. Their dog, Elliott, a stray that they had adopted, barked an excited greeting as we entered the house.

To the right, in the joint living room and dining room, the dining table took up most of the space. On the couch, against the wall under the stairs and facing the television, their cat, Couscous, slept curled up on a crocheted blanket. She too was rescued from the animal shelter.

Once inside, our first surprise was that the little boy held by the American soldier in the photo on the banner that we had seen everywhere *was* Gilbert. And his friend, Georgette, Madame Bisson's granddaughter, was the little girl in the poster. An American soldier had sent the snapshot back for the fiftieth anniversary and Gilbert had recognized himself. It was the only photo he had from his childhood.

A large framed copy of the poster sat on a shelf behind the table. Gilbert described how he saw the banners and couldn't believe that it was he and Georgette. The photo also led to a reunion with Georgette, who had been lost to him since the war. Georgette, like Gilbert, still lived in Normandy. On the wall behind the couch, another framed photo of their grandsons, Romain and Benoît, had the place of honor.

Gilbert carried our suitcases up the narrow wooden stairs and placed them in the guest room where Heather and I were to sleep. The simple, clean room, with ironed, embroidered sheets and pillowcases, had a crucifix over the bed, a television and a metal clothes rack.

When we came back down, Gilbert opened a bottle of chilled champagne and we sat out in the garden to sip it and to chat. The conversation felt light and friendly. We had the whole evening ahead and the next day to talk. I mentioned that it was Dad's birthday and we toasted him together. How perfect that I had found Gilbert on Dad's special day. Dad had celebrated his thirtieth birthday in France, with Gilbert. Now Gilbert and I were remembering Dad together on what would have been his eightieth.

Gilbert was retired from his job and spent his days tending a huge plot in a community vegetable garden nearby. Each day he brought home a basket of freshly harvested produce and Huguette made a fresh *potage*, or vegetable soup, for the first course of their dinner.

Huguette worked in a nearby hospital in the accounting office and had left work early that day to meet us in Caen. Somehow she had prepared a delicious dinner, the *potage* and a green salad from Gilbert's garden, *Coquilles Sainte-Jacques*, with seafood fresh from the nearby Atlantic, bread and wine, with a cheese board for dessert. After dinner, she brought out a box of chocolates and a dusty bottle of Calvados, the local hard cider, which I remembered Dad describing as "firewater."

Cathy, Gilbert's daughter, and her two small sons, Benoît, five, and Romain, nine, joined us in the evening for dinner. I told them all about the article I'd written for the 50th anniversary, how I'd sent it to the French Consulate, and how the press attaché had encouraged me to place the ad. We all marveled again at our good fortune to be together.

As we sat and chatted, crowded into their cozy living and dining room, I was grateful that my reunion with Gilbert came at the end of the trip. I'd had three-and-a-half weeks to let French seep into my brain and my heart, to listen, to learn, to speak and be understood.

As we talked, I realized that all the years of French classes and videos and countless hours studying vocabulary and irregular verbs had been for this moment, so that I could find and communicate with Gilbert DesClos and his family. I saw then that my ongoing passion for French and France had a deeper purpose than I could have ever imagined. Thank God I had held onto my dream. I knew that Dad would have been so proud—and amazed.

Gilbert asked questions about Dad, about our lives and about how Dad had died. When I told him that I had grown up hearing the stories about him and that Dad had talked about him again just before he died, Gilbert looked away and tried to compose himself, but couldn't stop the tears. I could tell that for Gilbert, who had never been adopted, knowing that Dad had never forgotten him meant everything.

Gilbert told me about his lonely years in the orphanage, waiting and hoping that somehow, Dad would come back for him. Then, in his teens, a kind woman took him in to live with her family and her love and nurturing helped him to gain confidence and strength.

He went into the military, served time in Vietnam, then came home and worked in a factory job for many years. When he met and married his wife Huguette in his early twenties, and they had their daughter Cathy, life took on meaning and depth.

"My life began again with my family," he said. "It was the most important thing." I remembered the time in Hawaii when my dad had said the very same words. I shivered, feeling the power of meeting this man, such a link to my father.

He told me the same stories Dad had told, but from a child's perspective. He talked of his excitement upon visiting the Navy camp and his fascination with the huge ships, where they sometimes ate lunch if Dad was busy down at the beach. He told how he loved zipping around in the Jeep and that Dad had even taught him the basics of how to drive it.

He talked about how Dad carried a gun, a fact that Dad had never mentioned. Listening to his stories gave me back some more pieces of my father and I was grateful.

He described the wonder of the delicious food that fed his body, day after day. But the most important memory he had was how Dad's love had nurtured his spirit. Remembering Dad's strong arms around him, he wept again. We sat together, silent and moved, missing the father who had loved us both.

After dinner, Gilbert uncorked the dusty bottle of Calvados. As we sipped the powerful cider, he became more serious, and seemed to be getting up his courage to talk to me about something else. Didn't I know the whole story already? I'd heard it so many times from Dad and now from Gilbert.

But nothing could have prepared me for what Gilbert was about to tell me.

Gilbert took a gulp of his Calvados, leaned forward and told me his version of that late October day in 1944, when he and Dad had to say goodbye.

Dad knelt down and held him close. Gilbert hung on tight, sobbing and burying his head in Dad's thick, wool Navy coat. Cold October winds whipped around them as men rushed by, carrying their heavy sea bags on their shoulders, excited to be going home.

It was time to say goodbye. As Dad stood up, Gilbert clung tight to his legs. Dad looked out at the waiting ship, then turned and spoke to Gilbert.

"Do you want to go home with me to America?" Dad asked.

Gilbert murmured "*Oui.*"

Dad picked him up and hoisted him onto his hip, as he'd done so many times and held him tight as they hopped into a Jeep for the trip down to the beach. As they boarded the ship, the captain, who'd been watching, shook his head.

"Johnson, off the record, if you're caught, I know nothing about this."

Dad nodded, shifting Gilbert's weight.

Within the hour, storm winds raged. Twenty-foot waves lashed the hull of the huge ship. They would not be able to cross the English Channel until the seas calmed. The storm lasted throughout the day and night.

The next morning, as the sun rose, the wind slackened and sailors scurried about, readying the ship for departure. Moments before the ship was to cast off, French gendarmes pulled up on the beach, demanding to speak with the captain.

Madame Bisson had reported that her ward had not returned home and they were looking for him.

The captain called for my father. After a long, strained pause, the lieutenant appeared at the top of the gangplank, carrying the sleepy boy in his arms. Gilbert rubbed his eyes in the bright sunlight. When he saw the gendarmes, he hid his head and clung to Dad.

"*Non!*" he wailed, "*Non.*" Dad walked down the gangplank, then knelt down on the sand with Gilbert. The gendarmes had to pull the boy away.

Madame Bisson placed him in an orphanage that night.

Gilbert replaced the cork in the Calvados bottle.

"Your father said he would come back for me. I have been waiting for fifty years for some word from him."

I sat, stunned. First that Dad had taken Gilbert onto the ship. He had never told us that part of the story. Then that Dad had promised to come back. He had never mentioned that either.

The cat was awake now and enjoying being petted by Romain, who listened intently to the conversation, his eyes wide and his head turning back and forth between us. Benoît had fallen asleep on the couch, next to the dog. I took another sip of my Calvados, trying to absorb these new facts.

We sat together in an awkward silence until Cathy asked, "Why didn't he? Why didn't he come back?"

Her tone was not exactly hostile, but it also wasn't warm. I could see what she meant. If my father had risked taking Gilbert onto the ship and then promised to come back for him, how could he not have kept that promise? How could you let a child down like that? I couldn't think of what to say in English, let alone French.

Then after a moment, Cathy whispered, *"Le destin."* Destiny. It was Gilbert's destiny to stay in France and have his life there, so that he could marry Huguette, and Cathy could be born, and her sons.

We sat together in the small living room, feeling the mystery of life and how we can't always understand, until we look back, why things happen the way that they do. After Cathy and her sons left and Heather went up to bed, Huguette, Gilbert and I sat together, talking until late. When we said goodnight, Gilbert took my hands, his eyes bright with tears.

"I always knew that someday I would hear from your father, that someone would come," he said. "Thank you."

We stood for a moment, both moved and grateful for the destiny that had brought us together. I climbed the narrow wooden stairs to the guest bedroom where Heather lay sleeping and slipped into bed. The shutters on the old window rattled with a wind off the sea, as I lay awake, going over all that had happened that afternoon.

I'd found Gilbert DesClos. We were sleeping in his house. He remembered Dad, even told the same stories. All of that felt amazing and gave me another link to Dad, with this emotional connection from his past and the war.

But the rest of the story, about taking Gilbert onto the ship, that Dad had never talked about. How desperate he must have been, to take such a risk. And how—why—had he carried that secret for his whole life?

Why hadn't he told us? Had he wanted to hide that he'd been willing to defy the rules? And what about his promise to come back for Gilbert? He'd never mentioned that either. Was he ashamed that he didn't fulfill his promise? Was my mother against the idea and was it just another subject that they argued about at night, when they thought we couldn't hear?

I could see my father and Gilbert on that windy, desolate beach and imagine the tug of the gendarmes pulling a part of Dad's heart away as they took the boy. I punched my pillow into a new shape and stared at the rough wood beams in the ceiling.

Why hadn't I paid more attention to how important this had been to Dad? But then, Dad had kept the real heart of the story hidden, what Gilbert had just told me. If I'd known that, would I have realized the depth of their connection? And why hadn't I helped Dad to find Gilbert earlier, while there was still time for him to be there with us now?

As the clock ticked on the bedside table and the hours passed, I realized I could find no answers from the past. But I'd found Gilbert again. We could go forward from there.

There was an aura of Dad about Gilbert. I noticed it in the way he patiently explained a game to his grandson, in his pride in his garden's bounty and in the concern he showed that Heather and I knew our way back to Paris.

When we left the next afternoon, Gilbert insisted on driving ahead of us to the freeway onramp to make sure we took the right one. Then he pulled over and stood beside his car, waving till we were out of sight, oblivious to the cars whizzing by, his slight figure silhouetted against the sky.

Could he have known that's exactly what Dad would have done? How had he become so like him, when they'd been together only four months? It was as if their bond had been so deep that Gilbert had soaked up Dad and decided, "I will be like this man."

I wiped away more tears as I waved out the window and watched Gilbert getting smaller and smaller in the rear view mirror. When we said goodbye that day, I vowed that we would never lose touch again.

Dad had been unable to keep his promise. I would make sure that I kept mine.

18

Back in California, Heather and I shared all our adventures with my sister Sharon, who was thrilled that she had been able to play such an important role in our reunion with Gilbert.

I told her about Gilbert's stories from his child's perspective and how Dad had taken him onto the ship, intending to bring him back. And that Dad had promised to come back for Gilbert. She looked as surprised as I'd been about that new part of the story.

"Did Dad ever tell you that?" I asked.

"Never, not a word. Only that he tried to adopt Gilbert and cared about him."

"Why would Dad have kept that part of the story secret?" I asked.

"Maybe he was shocked at his own actions, at his own desperation and at the risk that he had taken," she said.

"I guess we'll never know." I shook my head.

The next time I saw my mother, I related Gilbert's story of being on the ship, ready to come back with Dad to America. Had Dad told her about that? She was sitting up in bed, doing a crossword puzzle, her favorite pastime.

"Yes, that is true," she said, not looking up. "The captain told him that if he got caught, that he was on his own." I couldn't believe that she had also known that part of the story and yet neither she nor Dad had ever mentioned it.

"But wouldn't he have gotten into trouble, just bringing Gilbert onto the ship like that?" I asked her.

"I'm sure he would have," she answered, turning to look up a word in her paperback dictionary. "But he must not have been thinking about that then."

I could tell by the sharp tone of her voice that she didn't want to discuss it any further.

"No, I guess not," I said.

How mysterious life is, I thought. A storm had changed the destinies of both Gilbert and my father, and then my life, too, because I had felt compelled to try and find him.

My mother's life as a single woman, especially as she got older, hadn't turned out quite as she may have planned. My father had been happily remarried, but my mother had not had a successful long-term relationship since their divorce. After I found Gilbert, I noticed that she put my father's Navy photo from 1944 on her bedside table again. She also started referring to herself as a widow.

But she seemed interested, not only that I'd found Gilbert, but in going to France on the next trip to meet him. The upcoming trip involved a big party, with her in the place of honor, then the spa, castles and Paris.

Gilbert and Huguette were very excited to meet my mother. After all, the woman who had been married to my father must be kind and loving just like him, right? Luckily, the language barrier and the distance helped keep that fantasy alive and I softened my mother's words when I translated her messages into French.

I kept my word to stay in touch with Gilbert and Huguette. We exchanged letters often, their responses in Huguette's neat, feminine handwriting. I could imagine them sitting at their dining room table and composing the letters together. We chatted on the phone from time to time to talk and for birthdays—Gilbert's and mine were one day apart.

That first Christmas, everyone at Huguette's work chipped in to buy them a fax machine so that we could exchange letters faster, without the week to ten days that mail took to travel between California and France. I bought a fax machine too.

We exchanged simple Christmas gifts. Huguette sent me a cross-stitched tree ornament, which we placed on our tree. It felt right to include them in our thoughts during our family celebrations.

The next spring, 1995, my article about traveling for the month with Heather, "Two for the Road," came out in a major newspaper travel section in California, on Mother's Day. On the 50th anniversary of V.E. day, or Victory in Europe Day that same month, my story "Finding Gilbert" also came out in several newspapers, describing the emotional reunion with my French "brother."

I sent a copy to the press attaché at the French Consulate in San Francisco, thanking her for her part in helping me to find Gilbert. I also sent a copy to Gilbert and Huguette, knowing an English-speaking friend could translate it for them. In my correspondence with Gilbert and his wife, we were planning a special reunion and *fête* (celebration) in France, June 1996. My mother and my sister Sharon were planning to go, and Heather wanted to come again too.

147

After the reunion in Normandy with Gilbert, I planned an itinerary where we visited the spa near their home for five days of the seawater treatments we had so loved. Then a rail/drive trip, which included Mont Saint-Michel, touring the *châteaux* country and spending three nights in a castle. Then back up to Paris on the train, with some time for shopping and sightseeing. A close friend and her daughter were joining us for the tour after the reunion.

The night before our departure, I received an envelope from the travel agent with Eurail passes for Heather and me. I was sitting on my bed, going over the last minute packing details when I heard my father's voice clearly in my head, saying one of his favorite sayings: *Check and double check.* My eyes fell on the envelope from the travel agent again.

All right Dad, I will check, I half-groaned, laughing at the same time that I seemed to be listening to him "from the other side." But when I opened the envelope, I gasped. Somehow, I had the rail passes for my friend and her daughter—she had Heather's and mine. Thank goodness I had checked.

Heather and I were leaving ahead of the others and couldn't have used rail passes that didn't match our passports. My friend and her daughter's rail passes would have also been invalid. That would have meant a huge loss of money, not to mention the confusion of having to buy train tickets; my friend didn't speak French. Instead, a quick phone call and it all got sorted out in minutes.

Thank you, Dad, I mumbled, truly grateful and in awe that I'd heard him like that. Did he know that we were going back to see Gilbert? Such mystery.

Gilbert and his family created a moving and memorable fête in our honor. Fifty of their friends and relations came out for a whole day of feasting and celebrating in the decorated town hall of their village. The mayor showed up to shake hands and share a glass of champagne. The newspaper, *Ouest France*, sent a reporter who scribbled down names and facts and took photos.

I translated for my mother, Heather and Sharon practiced their French and we laughed and smiled all day. It was a wonder to see how much Gilbert's friends and extended family shared his delight at finally finding his American family and how much the story meant to them, too.

For Gilbert, it was the fulfillment of a dream to meet my mother and Sharon, two more members of his American family and to share the wonder of our reunion with his family and friends. My mother was honored as Dad's wife; although Gilbert and Huguette knew about my parents' divorce, no one mentioned it.

We gathered in the late morning for champagne. Then about noon we sat down to eat. Sharon, Mom and I sat at a head table with Gilbert and Huguette. Huguette, with help from a few friends, orchestrated the serving of course after course from the kitchen in the hall.

The village of Colombelles is located just a few kilometers from the Atlantic, so we enjoyed many courses of *fruits de mer*, fresh seafood, which I learned the words for—mussels, *les moules*, lobster, *homard*, clams, *les palourdes*, oysters, *les huîtres*, and crab, *du crabe*. Those creatures were swimming in the English Channel just hours before they ended up on our plates.

Huguette had been cooking for weeks and storing food at her neighbors' homes. Quiches, hors d'oeuvres, salads, tarts. Friends brought dishes that they'd created, including varied and luscious desserts—cakes, crêpes and ice cream.

We brought presents for the family and Gilbert's grandsons, Romain, now eleven and Benoît, seven, loved their "Wilson" t-shirts so much that they promptly put them on over their formal clothes. I filled my head with the language while my belly filled with champagne and food and my heart with all the love that was pouring out to us.

People moved about and chatted with each other between courses. Gilbert made several speeches and toasts, with glasses raised and much cheering. Children ran around on the grass outside. At three o'clock in the afternoon, we all stood to take a breather before the dessert course.

Heather, at twenty-one, sat with the young people, talking and laughing. After our trip two years before, when we found Gilbert, she spent six weeks the following summer in Annecy, staying with a family. This was now her third trip to France in three years and she spoke French well.

By five o'clock, many of the guests had left, but a smaller core group remained. My sister and Heather joined my mother back at the house, so I was the only member of the family still at the fête. Though hard to imagine, there was to be another light meal that evening.

It really is a wonder how the French stay so slim. But I wanted to stay to the very end to honor all their efforts. Gilbert, Huguette and I headed back to their home about nine that night.

When the newspaper article came out in *Ouest France* later that week, the headline read, *"Sa famille Américaine est enfin arrivée."* His American family has finally arrived. Gilbert beamed at the article, which included a photo of us all lined up on the grass outside the town hall.

Mom, Sharon, Heather and I stayed with Gilbert and Huguette for an extra week, with Gilbert acting as our chauffeur, driving us each morning to the spa and picking us up each afternoon. Huguette coddled and cared for us, preparing breakfast and dinner each day. Many days, she packed us a lunch to take with us for our noon meal. We sat on the beach and savored cheese, bread, cold cuts and fruit, and sipped wine.

Heather and I were thrilled to be back again where we'd been two years before. Gilbert and Huguette joined us at the spa on the last day to soak in the warm seawater pools.

During our stay, Gilbert took us to the house he had lived in with Madame Bisson and Georgette, just above the camp. That day, we also visited the American Cemetery again—such a powerful and moving experience.

Gilbert and Huguette had purchased an English/French dictionary, which sat on top of the television, right next to the dining table. When we reached a word that I didn't know, I'd look it up and show it to them and then we'd all smile, another piece of understanding reached between us. Most of the time we did well, but having the dictionary helped. They still spoke only a few words of English, "hello," "goodbye" and "thank you."

On our last day, Gilbert and Huguette drove us to the train station to begin the rail and drive trip that I'd so carefully planned. The one glitch, however, was that the trains didn't run to Mont Saint-Michel that day. We sat at the train station, with no train to board, trying to figure out what to do. Then Gilbert and Huguette volunteered to drive us the one-and-a-half-hour drive, even though it meant they each drove one of their cars, to take us all.

At Mont Saint-Michel, we spent the day together climbing the narrow cobblestone streets to the church at the top, marveling at the dramatic views from the steep stone ramparts down to the sea below. Late in the afternoon, we all shared a coffee in a café and then it was time to say goodbye. After tearful kisses all around, Gilbert and Huguette headed back home. The next morning, the six of us boarded the train to begin our trip through the *châteaux* country and then back to Paris.

I called Gilbert and Huguette from Paris for one last goodbye and thank you for such a warm and welcoming visit. We were already planning their visit to California the following spring.

Gilbert was finally making his trip to America.

Part V

1997

19

We stayed in contact by fax and phone, as we planned their two-week visit for the following spring, April 1997. They were coming with their daughter Cathy and Romain and Benoît. Our whole family buzzed with excitement as we arranged the many dinners, picnics and gatherings to celebrate them.

We were gathering both in Northern and Southern California, with the bigger events in the south, where most of the family lived.

In April, I met the DesClos family at the airport in San Francisco and began a fun-filled tour of the city. We took the glass elevator at the Hyatt in Union Square, gasping as we whizzed up on the outside of the building and marveling at the views of the city and San Francisco Bay. We hopped onto the cable cars, toured Fisherman's Wharf, and walked through Chinatown, spending two days in the city to be sure to have time to take in all the sights.

They felt right at home at the Boudin bakery where we found "real" French *baguettes*, then savored their first American hamburgers at a fifties diner, where Romain and Benoît wiggled with excitement at the free cardboard "classic car" gifts that came with their meal.

They gasped as we drove down Lombard Street, known as the "crookedest street in the world," then over the Golden Gate Bridge to Sausalito and Marin County, where we lunched with a dear friend in her eighties who had lived in Paris in the 1930's. Then home to Nevada City, in the foothills of the Sierras, where we relaxed for a week's stay.

In Nevada City, a California Gold Rush town that dates back to the 1850's, they stayed at a bed and breakfast, right on the quaint main street, exploring the historical town and all the shops, when we weren't off on excursions.

We took picnics to the Yuba River, appreciating the colorful spring wild flowers, and toured the Empire goldmine in the area. My sister and her family drove them to Lake Tahoe for the day and on another night, we shared a family dinner at a restaurant in town, thirteen of us in all.

My nephew Brendan and Gilbert's grandson Romain were both twelve, and Romain wanted to visit Brendan's school. After sitting in the classroom and touring the school, Romain joined in a soccer game at recess. By the end of the visit, Romain declared that he wanted to come to live in California—he thought that the schools were much less formal than in France and the kids had way more fun.

Just before Gilbert and Huguette arrived, my sweet elderly neighbors who owned the beautiful apple farm just up the hill passed away. By a miraculous series of events, I was able to buy the farm and was in escrow. We walked the property together and looked it over and Gilbert offered to come back and help me with the work needed to restore it. I so appreciated his offer.

Our last evening in Nevada City, we gathered at a friend's home for a farewell party. About thirty friends came with food, several played guitars and we sang, ate and celebrated. Some folks dusted off their college French and other times, I translated for our French family, who appreciated the warmth of it all.

For the hour-long trip to the Sacramento airport the next morning, my friend Sarah rented us a limousine. We all piled in, marveling at the luxurious fun of sipping champagne as we whizzed along. Romain and Benoît especially enjoyed the fun as the eleven of us traveled together to join the rest of the family in the south.

As I sat next to Gilbert for the short flight to San Diego, he tapped his sugar packet on one side, then turned it over and tapped it again on the other side, before adding it to his coffee. I had never seen anyone do that except my dad.

In La Jolla, where my mother lived, the rest of the extended family, forty members in all and spanning four generations, gathered for the weekend to welcome and honor our French family. At one picnic, we all played soccer— Gilbert and my brothers, my nephews and his grandsons, Heather and I—the international game needing no translation.

At a formal dinner hosted by my mother, Gilbert stood up and, with shaking hands, read a letter he'd composed. I stood next to him and held his other hand, translating his words for him. He thanked everyone, remembering Dad and expressing his wonder at finally fulfilling his dream to come to America and meet his family. Even my mother cried during the touching speech.

As we all talked and visited after dinner, Gilbert's grandsons and my three nephews, similar in age and tired of all the formality, jumped into the community pool at my mother's condominium complex, right outside where we were gathered.

157

The boys whooped and hollered as they romped and splashed in their underwear, their clothes piled up alongside the pool. We all giggled, enjoying their exuberance, even though we had to shush them a bit—it was after hours for the pool.

While in the San Diego area, we visited Sea World and kissed dolphins, and drove across the bay to Coronado Island. We rode the trolley down to Tijuana, Mexico for the day, where Cathy demonstrated a distinct talent at bargaining for turquoise jewelry. They sampled their first Mexican food, the spicy tacos and enchiladas tasting a bit strange to them, but relished the novelty of being able to journey to Mexico and back in one day.

After San Diego, we headed north to Los Angeles. They wanted to see Beverly Hills, so we drove down Rodeo drive and through the neighborhoods of expensive homes, then past the Hollywood sign, which they had seen in so many movies.

We spent another day squealing on the rides and marveling at the behind-the-scenes technology of movie making at Universal Studios.

At my brother Kenton's house one afternoon, his sons and Gilbert's grandsons, the pool-caper culprits reunited, ran past the adults, giggling and excited. As we chatted and sipped tea and coffee, they played basketball, then swam in the pool and played Nintendo.

Finally, Romain and Benoît dressed up in my nephews' baseball uniforms, proudly showing us all, and tried their hands at baseball. Once again, it didn't seem to matter that the boys didn't speak each other's language. They were speaking the universal language of being boys, of fun and youthful enthusiasm.

As Gilbert and his family took it all in, I witnessed America and California through their eyes—our huge freeways, our giant American cars and trucks, our contrasts of wide-open spaces and dense cities, our fast-paced life—and saw it all newly.

Their return flight left from Los Angeles, so after our busy and joyous two weeks we said goodbye, promising to see each other soon, our connection deeper and more solid.

We were a true family now. Their three French generations had joined with our four American generations in a strong bond of love and understanding that bridged language and cultural differences.

20

The following spring, 1998, I returned to France in early June, to visit Gilbert and Huguette and to write more articles. I hadn't packed a raincoat and got caught in a storm walking to the train station. By the time I arrived at their home, damp and bedraggled, I had a bad cold. Huguette took one look at me, clucked like a mother hen and announced, "*Je m'occupe de toi*." I'm going to take care of you.

She bundled me into the car and drove to the shopping center near their home to buy me a raincoat. After cruising through a few stores, we found a nice blue and green coat and I tried it on. She made me turn around, pulling on it, making sure it fit just right, then insisted on paying for it.

Back home, she coddled me with warm drinks and scolded me into naps. It felt delicious and sweet. I'd never been mothered like that and I left feeling closer to them than ever.

As I celebrated my fiftieth birthday that fall, hitting the half-century point woke me up to my unfulfilled and long-buried dream of living in France. As 1998 turned over into 1999, the last year before the new millennium, I felt the strong stirrings of that dream surface again. My French was strong, thanks to all the visits with Gilbert and Huguette.

Could it still be possible? Was there a way? And if not now, when?

In 1999, as I considered the possibility of living in France, I was invited on two trips to France, in January and again in May, to research and write travel articles. Counting my trip in 1998, I'd been there three times in twelve months and the longing to live there increased.

I set the intention that by fall, I would begin my "junior year abroad, thirty years late" and celebrate the new millennium living in France for as many months as I could arrange.

On the spring trip, I spent two days in Aix-en-Provence, near Marseilles, walking the winding cobblestone streets that led to the central square, with its 13th century clock tower that tolled the hour. Over fifty fountains flowed throughout the city.

This is where I would live when I come to stay, I decided. Though I knew no one there, it *felt right* and I trusted that. I returned home to set my plan in motion.

The months, weeks and days sped by and my proposed date to leave, November 3rd, loomed ahead. For my eight-month stay in France, I found a renter for my house, bought a laptop, and put my bills online.

I had some clients that I could work with long distance and some articles lined up to write—enough work to just squeak by.

I said goodbye to family and friends and headed to San Francisco for the flight to Paris. The hardest part was saying goodbye to my new little granddaughter, Ellie, my first grandchild. But my son-in-law Claude encouraged me to not put off the trip any longer.

"You have your whole life to be a grandma," he said. "You should go."

He was right. He and my daughter Michelle promised to come over for a visit in the spring. I took one compact rolling bag, and a small backpack. Why take clothes to France, the fashion capital of the world, I thought?

As the big jet lumbered down the runway, then rose into the sky, I could see San Francisco below and the Golden Gate Bridge off in the distance. What a beautiful city. At that moment, I felt a stab of fear. What was I doing, leaving everything and everyone behind—my home, my friends, and my family—a perfectly good life, in search of a dream?

Then tears of relief trickled down my cheeks. I was on my way. And Gilbert and his family waited for me there, my family, in France.

Darkness came early to the City of Light in November and I struggled the first few days with both jet lag and the fact that I'd opted to stay in a youth hostel/dormitory for foreign students, where I felt out of place. I was on an emotional roller coaster, high and excited one minute, then cold and lonely the next, especially in the chilly Paris evenings.

I solved one part of the problem by investing in a long, black, wool coat that not only made me fit in like a Parisian, but also kept me warm against the frigid winds blowing along Boulevard Saint-Germain. One evening, on my way back to the hostel, something caught my eye in a shop window and I slowed down to look. Three words stood out against the backdrop of the window display.

"*Croire en soi.*" Believe in yourself. I stopped and looked closer at the window—a bookstore, with textbooks, notebooks and school supplies. The words didn't seem to be related to anything in particular, but if there were any three words I needed at that moment, they were, "*Croire en soi.*"

Believing in myself meant trusting that I would find a home, friends, and a life in France for the next eight months. That I could trust myself, life, destiny—everything that had brought me to that exact moment, standing alone on a chilly corner in Paris, just weeks before the new millennium.

People bustled by, heading home with their fresh *baguettes*, cars honked and the wind blew golden leaves around the sidewalk. I stared at the words and let them sink in deep. If my eyes had been just a few inches higher or lower, if I had glanced away, I would have missed them.

But I didn't miss them. They would become my mantra as I stepped into my new life in France and from then on.

"Croire en soi."

A few days later, I took the #21 bus across Paris to the Gare Saint-Lazare and caught the train to Normandy to visit Gilbert and Huguette. The comfort and familiarity of their warm home felt like a balm. We celebrated our two birthdays—Gilbert's and mine being only one day apart. They were excited that I was staying in France for eight months, giving us lots of chances to visit each other.

Gilbert liked to tease me, calling me *"notre petite Américaine,"* our little American. I take after my Dad and at almost five foot eleven, am a good four inches taller than Gilbert. I had to sleep at an angle in their guest bed and duck going up their wooden stairs to avoid bumping my head.

I knew that they were thrilled to see me each time I visited. My presence must have brought back memories of not only Dad, but also of all the good times we'd shared since our reunion. They had a video of their visit to California and we watched it together, laughing and remembering all of the special moments.

Huguette was worried that I was going south to a city where I knew no one and invited me to stay with them for my time in France. I considered her offer, but knew I needed to believe in myself and have the experience of finding my own way. I trusted that I was drawn to the south of France and Aix-en-Provence, so thanked her and reassured her that we could see each other and talk on the phone often.

I traveled back to Paris, then south on the train to Marseilles, to transfer to Aix-en-Provence. As the fast train sped south, rain spattered against the windows and clouds changed shape as the sky turned from gray to blue. I snuggled up in my long, black wool coat and took a nap, waking up just as we pulled into Marseilles. I found the smaller, local train to Aix, then walked the fifteen minutes to my hotel, pulling my rolling bag.

Over the next few weeks, I discovered that finding an apartment was much harder than I had expected. In Aix, a university town, thousands of students had arrived months before, snagging all the best places. I called ad after ad from phone booths and looked at dark and dingy rooms above tattoo parlors, in basements, or on busy streets. Nothing felt right.

I wanted sunlight, windows and a bathtub—a place where I could write and feel renewed—and I wasn't going to settle for less. I was using up my resources staying in a hotel, but I had to trust and wait.

I found a group of British and American expatriates who met weekly for coffee and conversation. As much as I loved the challenge of speaking French, it was fun for that brief time to speak my native tongue.

A new French friend from the group Maïté, who came to practice her English, told me about an apartment in the old part of town, *"centre-ville,"* a great location for walking to everything. She didn't know all the details, but gave me the phone number.

The next morning, the real estate agent and I met at the apartment and walked up the three flights of stairs, to the door on the left. The big rusty key turned in the lock and the door swung open to sunlight blazing through tall windows in the kitchen and living room. In the dining room, French doors opened to a tiny balcony. I turned the corner off the kitchen to the bathroom and saw a deep, old bathtub.

Sunlight, windows and a bathtub. I took a breath and smiled at the woman.

"I'll take it!" I said.

21

The apartment was partially furnished, meaning that it had furniture, but no towels, sheets or kitchen items. Maïté loaned me some kitchen things and drove me to a huge *supermarché*, where I bought sheets, towels and pillows. I put my new linens on the bed, hung the dishtowels in the kitchen, then took a long, hot soak in my bathtub, drying off with my fresh, new towels.

After heating some soup in my one saucepan, I put out the *baguette*, cheese and wine that I'd bought, set the table with my borrowed dishes and sat down for my first meal there. Then I snuggled into my cozy bed and drifted off to sleep. I was home. In France.

I left a few days later to take the train north to spend Christmas with Gilbert and Huguette. Storms had been raging all over France—the Seine was flooding in Paris and huge trees had fallen, stopping many trains. But my time in Normandy was quiet and sweet.

On Christmas Eve, Cathy and her sons came over to exchange gifts and we turned on the tiny tree in the window, with the bright colored lights. Huguette prepared a special feast of roast chicken and we sipped champagne and toasted the new millennium that was just days away. It felt so comforting to be "home for Christmas" with my family, in France.

As always, Huguette showed concern that I was all right in my life in the south, and told me again that I could come and stay with them for as long as I wanted or needed to. I reassured her that I was fine, especially now that I had found such a wonderful apartment.

Huguette's caring and concern reminded me so much of my dad. Gilbert had found and married a woman who treated others with the same warmth and love as my father had. We planned for them to come and visit me in the spring and I was coming back to see them again in late January. They were my safety net, just a phone call and a train ride away.

I returned to Aix three days before the millennium, walking the short distance from the train station to my apartment and up the three flights of stairs. I stood at my front door, jiggling the key in the lock, just so, a little up and to the right and click, the old door creaked open. I peeked in, tentative at first—I'd heard that apartments got broken into a lot in France and I'd been gone for a week.

But it looked just as it had when I rushed out to catch the train to Paris. The hand-embroidered tablecloth I'd picked up at the open market for 28 francs, or four dollars, covered the weathered pine table. A slender purple iris, in a vase made of a blue glass juice bottle with the label soaked off, stood in the center. All was quiet.

I crept in, the cool tiles echoing my footsteps. My dishes drained on the counter in the new, white plastic dish drainer I'd bought just before I left. The cold air made me shiver, from no heat for a week and the frigid December nights and chilly mistral winds, which rattled the doors and windows.

The late afternoon sunlight streamed in and reflected off the gold plastered walls and the orange floor tiles. As I moved around the corner to the bedroom to put down my suitcase, I let out the breath I didn't know I'd been holding.

Safe in my own apartment, I kept pinching myself. I was living in France, making a life, finding my way. With six months left of my adventure, what lay ahead? I felt breathless to find out.

As the New Year unfolded, my days took on an easy rhythm. I walked to the open-air market to buy just-picked fruits and vegetables. The carrots tasted sweeter, the apples tart and the cherries more luscious than any I had ever known. The fruits that weren't grown locally came from Africa, reminding me how far I was from home. The large brown eggs, gathered from plump *Provençal* hens and displayed in a basket, still had downy feathers stuck to them.

In California, I had used an organizer for twenty years to plan my days. Here I relaxed and allowed the days to unfold. I learned to hang out. I spent whole afternoons at cafés with friends, where we engaged in spirited discussions, then went to a movie or dinner.

Other times, I sat alone and watched people or wrote, feasting my senses on the sound of water splashing in a fountain or sunlight slanting off a medieval building.

I appreciated the ritual of the more formal manners of the French. Entering the local bakery for my evening *baguette à l'ancienne*, an ancient recipe baguette, I was greeted warmly. Leaving, I traded salutations with the shopkeepers again, *Merci, bonsoir*. As I headed home to my apartment, the bread, still warm from the wood-fired oven, felt alive in my hands.

Walking everywhere kept me in shape, in spite of the *croissants* and *pain au chocolat* I consumed. Weekends, I hiked with my new friends up to the top of Mont Sainte-

Victoire, the nearby peak painted by Cézanne, or along the jagged cliffs above the Mediterranean.

Life without a car felt carefree, unburdened by the hassles of parking, petrol, toll roads, or rental fees. I was able to go wherever I wanted by foot, bus, train or by hitching a ride with friends.

Aix was founded by the Romans because of a *source* or thermal spring. The site of the spring now was a spa, offering mud wraps, massages and baths at a reasonable price. I signed up for a series of treatments and went each week.

By February, the pure immersion of living in France for almost four months was paying off. I was at lunch at Maïté's and as everyone chattered in rapid French, I realized I could understand and respond, without thinking. Maïté congratulated me on my new ease and confidence in the language. I called Gilbert and Huguette often, never getting over the thrill of being in the same country and time zone.

I wrote and sold articles about my experiences living in France, including one to *More* magazine, entitled "My French Affaire, How I Did my Junior Year Abroad Thirty Years Late." It was a gift to have so much to write about and the time to do it.

In May, my daughter Michelle, her husband Claude and my nine-month-old granddaughter Ellie came over to visit. By then, I could switch back and forth from French to English like changing channels on the radio, a thrill that I'd waited almost forty years to achieve.

Gilbert and Huguette came and stayed during that time and we all enjoyed a special visit together. They applauded my apartment and how I'd settled in so well. I slept in the living room on a foldout couch and gave them my bedroom. It felt good to reciprocate their hospitality, in my own place, in France.

Just as I had mixed feelings when I arrived in France, I had similar feelings when it was time to return home. I had discovered a better quality of life there—my rent was lower, food was more reasonable and fresh, I lived without the expense of a car and savored the slower pace of life. I felt softer speaking French and reveled in the rhythm and elegance of the language.

In my eight-month stay, I discovered that I could create a life from nothing, in a foreign language and end up landing on my feet. My success in finding my sunny apartment, meeting great friends and my new fluency in French gave me a stronger and more certain sense of myself. I loved visiting Gilbert and Huguette and being more a part of their lives.

But with my family and now a grandchild in America, I didn't want to be so far away. Most importantly, as I looked back on my time in France, it felt like I had reached back in time and pulled that nineteen-year-old forward, reclaiming parts of myself at a deep level. I was grateful that I had been able to slow down, reevaluate my life and then come more into the present as I began the second half-century of my life.

Before my stay in France, my sister Sharon had been diagnosed with brain tumors and during my time in France, she had been relatively stable. But when I returned, her condition became more serious and I was glad to be back to help in her care. Two-and-a-half years after my return, she died at home, surrounded by her children, family and a few close friends. Sharon's battle was over, but I struggled with the reality that she was gone. She had not only been my sister, but played the role of the loving and nurturing mother that my mother had never been able to play.

I had kept in touch with Gilbert and Huguette throughout Sharon's illness and Huguette and I cried together when I told her about Sharon's death. I'd been so caught up in helping my sister that I'd not been able to visit them since returning from France in 2000. The 60th anniversary of D-Day was coming up the next year in June 2004. I set a goal to go.

On a whim, I contacted Stephen Ambrose Historical Tours to see if they needed any tour guides or translators for their anniversary tours. I sent them my articles and qualifications and they called me back and said 'yes, I was hired'.

I would accompany a group of U.S. Army Rangers in France for the anniversary. I was thrilled. I made arrangements to go a week early to spend time with Gilbert and Huguette before the tour began and also to have some time to visit with them again after.

With my trip lined up, on another hunch, I sent a proposal to the local National Public Radio station about doing a series of commentaries for the upcoming anniversary. The manager of the station called me right back, excited. "You have no idea how rare it is to have something of this quality come across my desk," he said. Another chance to be thrilled.

In the months before my trip, I traveled to the Seabee Museum and archives at Point Mugu Naval Base, north of Los Angeles, hoping to gather some new information about Dad's time in France. After getting a security clearance to come onto the base, I sat down in a room with seven large cardboard filing boxes of artifacts from my father's battalion, the 111th Seabee Naval Construction Battalion, from 1943-1945.

For hours, on the first morning, I sifted through the boxes of papers, disappointed to find nothing related to Dad.

Then I saw some neat fine printing from a report of the "officer of the day." At the end of it was my father's signature, *Lieutenant Donald K. Johnson.* I held the paper close to my heart, knowing that Dad had signed it sixty years before.

In the next box, I came across a grainy black-and-white photo of a group of sailors lined up in a field in Normandy. Dad stood straight and tall at one end, in his officer's uniform and hat. He was not smiling.

What was he thinking and feeling that day? Was that photo taken near the end, when Dad knew that he couldn't bring Gilbert home with him? Was Gilbert waiting at the side, just outside of the photograph, for Dad to finish? I so wished I could have jumped into the scene and followed him around and asked him all the questions that I now knew to ask.

There were photos of the tents, lined up in neat rows, in the camp on the cliff above Omaha Beach. In another photo, men sat in a field attending Catholic Mass, the priest in front in his long robes. I searched in the crowd for Dad, but didn't find him there.

I found papers listing different projects that Dad had worked on in the surrounding areas. He and his team spent over a week in Bayeux, doing some restoration. I learned that Dad had been one of the officers in charge of building the Rhino Ferries in England in the months leading up to the invasion and learned more about the important part the ferries, called "a secret weapon of the invasion," played on D-Day and beyond.

I saw the hand-written lists of assignments for the D-Day invasion, with my father's name, then "D-Day plus one," Omaha Beach. I took in a quick breath, knowing again the good fortune that gave him the orders to land the day after D-Day on "Bloody Omaha."

As I sat in the room surrounded by the dusty boxes and papers of my father's battalion, I could feel him there, in France, in the life he had experienced before I was born, the life that included Gilbert, who had now been my French brother for almost ten years.

22

I arrived in Paris and took the train from Gare Saint-Lazare to Normandy, a journey I had made so many times before, to visit Gilbert and Huguette. As always, when the train pulled into the station in Caen, Gilbert waited in the crowd to meet me. He waved and smiled, giving me the special 'four kisses on the cheeks' of welcome, then pulled my bag along to their car.

"*Ça va Diane?*" he asked. Everything going well?

Back at their cozy home, we shared the warm meal that Huguette had prepared, then they shooed me off to bed to rest and recover from my jet lag. We spent the next relaxing days together enjoying Huguette's delicious food and catching up on the time that had passed since our last visit together in France in 2000. At the end, I felt rested and ready for the upcoming tour.

All of Normandy hummed with excitement for the big anniversary. It would be the last one that many of the Veterans, now in their late seventies and early eighties, would be able to attend. The presidents of America and France and the Chancellor of Germany would all attend the formal ceremony on June 6th at the American cemetery at Colleville-sur-Mer.

After my time with Gilbert and Huguette, I returned to Paris, rounded up my sweet Veterans and their families at the airport and we all boarded the bus to head back to Normandy. My group, seven members of the elite Army Rangers, had scaled the one-hundred-foot cliff, Pointe du Hoc, on the morning of D-Day, straight up into the fury of the Germans.

I did some research on the Rangers and felt in awe of what they faced and overcame on D-Day. As they scaled the cliff, the Germans at the top shot down at them, cut their ropes, threw back their ladders and dropped grenades and boulders down on them. Of the two-hundred-forty Rangers who began the ascent up the cliff, one-hundred-eighty made it to the top to face hand-to-hand combat.

They defeated those Germans, then, found and destroyed five big enemy guns that were pounding the beaches below. That act alone saved thousands of American lives on D-Day and beyond. By the time the Rangers were relieved two days later, ninety-one had been killed and fifty-nine wounded. Ninety were able to continue to fight. D-day and the days following, the residents of the nearby villages welcomed the Rangers with open arms. They shared food and champagne, but especially their gratitude.

These same villages had never stopped welcoming returning Rangers through the years. Of the seven Rangers returning for the 60th anniversary, one man had returned with family members every five years, though most had not been back since 1944.

When we arrived in Normandy, French and American flags hung from windows everywhere. People stopped and waved when our bus, with the words "American Army Rangers" on the side, went by.

The villagers treated the Veterans like honored guests. At one small ceremony in a village square, the French and American national anthems alternated, playing out of a tinny sound system set up in a van. But you could feel the heart that went into all the preparations. The French and the Veterans were grateful for my translating and we'd stand together, moved and touched, wiping away tears.

Our group attended a special mass in the first village liberated by the Rangers in 1944. All ages, from tiny children to elderly grandparents, crowded into the church and stood up in respect when we walked in.

The elders had passed the stories down to their children and grandchildren, telling about the brave young men who landed and saved them on that June morning sixty years before. Afterwards, we sipped champagne and ate sweet butter cookies together outside on the lawn.

The Veterans jumped right into the celebrations, shaking hands, signing autographs and posing for photos. The sun was hot, the hours were long, the jet lag was hard, but they were in their glory and everyone wanted them to have it.

One of the French hosts spoke for many of the villagers when welcoming the Veterans: "Here in Normandy, we don't forget the heroes who liberated us in the last war, and those who died here. Here in Normandy, we will never forget."

On the afternoon of June 6th, the Army had arranged a special ceremony just for the Rangers. At this intimate and powerful event, the seven men stood at attention, saluting. Their shoulders were stooped with age; they couldn't stand as straight and tall as they had all those years before. But you could see the pride in the way they held themselves. You could see the soldiers they had been.

Afterwards, young army men and women thronged around to listen to them, to shake their hands and to be photographed with them. The Veterans were being rightfully honored as the heroes that they were.

The next day, I skipped a boat outing to the cliffs at Pointe du Hoc in order to call the National Public Radio station for an interview. As I left the phone booth, I noticed my group of Veterans and their families frantically waving their arms and yelling at me across the harbor. Something was clearly wrong.

As I gazed across the water between us, I realized I couldn't get to them without going around and it was way too far to walk or run. Starting to feel panicked myself, I flagged down a passing truck and asked if they could please drive me to the other side of the harbor. We sped over to the group.

One of the Veterans, Ivor, normally outgoing and energetic, lay unmoving in an ambulance. His son, who had traveled with him to the reunion, was in tears, helpless and unable to understand what was going on.

I sorted out that Ivor had had a stroke and that the paramedics were taking him to Bayeux, the closest hospital. A local offered to drive us, so we hopped into his car and followed the ambulance. No one at the hospital spoke English, so I agreed to help until Ivor could be transferred to the American hospital in Paris, where more of the staff spoke English.

It took three days to arrange the transfer and to make sure that Ivor was strong enough to make the drive to Paris in the ambulance. At the American hospital, he could rest and heal until he was able to withstand the long flight home.

He'd told his son over and over, "I just want to make it back to Normandy for the anniversary and reunion." He'd gotten his wish, but unfortunately, the day after, had a stroke. His son and I shook our heads at the irony of that. The day that they left for Paris, I stood by the ambulance to say goodbye and his son took my hands.

"Your father would have been so proud of you," he said. We both wiped away tears as we hugged goodbye.

After several more weeks in the hospital in Paris, Ivor healed enough to travel home. He lived another year before his son called to tell me that his father had died. The sixtieth anniversary and reunion had been one of the high points of his father's life and he had relived the pleasure of it over and over during his last months.

Helping them had been one of the most rewarding and moving experiences of my life and showed me, once again, the power of a language to bridge worlds. Gilbert picked me up for a short visit before I headed back to Paris and home and I shared with them many of my memories and powerful, moving moments from the tour.

Being with the Veterans and their families and witnessing the gratitude of the French towards the *vieux soldats*, the old soldiers, gave me another experience of my father's generation, whom Tom Brokaw called "The Greatest Generation." Here are the closing words of my final National Public Radio commentary recorded from the Paris N.P.R. office and sent back to the California station:

"My father's stories about the Normandy Invasion were not about war, per se, but about relationships. Sixty years later, I too will be telling stories about the relationships I experienced in Normandy, between the Veterans and their families, between the young and the old, between the French and the Americans.

Everyone has gone home now. The returning travelers will have stories to tell at their Veterans of Foreign War meetings. Their long-time friends will lean in close, hands cupped over their ears, to catch all the details of the powerful journey.

For the rest of us who were on the trip, we'll never forget that we were there with them, that one last time.

I think we're fascinated with World War II because it was a display of courage by so many ordinary men. In the face of danger and death, they did the right thing. Not only the right thing, the heroic thing.

I think we're fascinated with the story because we want to believe that we all have the capacity within us to be heroes, to be great, to be courageous, even in the face of death.

WWII Veterans are dying at the rate of one thousand per day. While they're still here with us, we have the chance to ask them questions and to listen. To thank them. They gave us so much. Now it's our turn to give back to them.

And if you look into their eyes, you can see who they were.

It's right there. You just have to look."

23

I kept in touch with Gilbert and Huguette with phone calls, letters and faxes. I had good intentions to return to France again but somehow three years passed without time for a trip back. During that time, I experienced the joy of the birth of three more grandchildren. My mother also passed away and though our relationship wasn't close, I'd been able to help her a lot at the end of her life.

Finally, in the fall of 2007, I began planning a month-long trip to France for February 2008. I arranged various assignments for articles and at the beginning of the trip, I set aside time to visit Gilbert and Huguette for a long visit. I hadn't been back since 2004 and so looked forward to spending time with them again.

In October, Huguette expressed concern that Gilbert had lost a lot of weight and he was going to have some tests to see if they could find out the cause. He was so healthy. Surely nothing could be wrong.

In November, Huguette called to tell me that Gilbert had been diagnosed with liver cancer. With treatment and rest, they felt hopeful that he could fight the disease. Huguette was retired and could take care of him. We talked on the phone often for updates but as the weeks passed, the news wasn't good; he was failing fast. I hoped and prayed that I could get there in time.

Hold on, I thought, as I packed and completed things for my upcoming trip. *I'm coming. Just a few more days now.* Sharon had held on for years; I prayed that Gilbert could last a few more weeks.

"Diane will be here soon," Huguette told him and he smiled and seemed comforted.

But he couldn't hold on. He died two weeks before I was scheduled to leave for France. Huguette and I cried together when she told me the news. After the phone call, I sat at my desk and stared out the window at the gray January sky, then called Huguette right back to find out the plans for the memorial.

As we spoke again, I knew it was completely unreasonable and maybe impossible, but I had to try to get there in time for his funeral. After a flurry of phone calls and condensing two weeks into a few hours, I left to drive to San Francisco to catch the next day's flight to Paris. If I traveled straight through, I might just make it.

The next afternoon, I settled into my seat on Air France for the long flight across the Atlantic. As we flew into the night, I felt grateful for the quiet as the other passengers slept all around me. But I couldn't sleep. After the shock of the news and all the rushing to leave, it was my first chance to stop and gather my thoughts.

I was on my way to Gilbert's funeral. The story that began almost sixty-four years before was now complete. Gilbert and my dad were both gone. And yet here I was, with my heart tangled up too, compelled to be there for Gilbert's funeral. Was that for me, or for my dad?

I didn't know. I only knew that I trusted the mysteries of life and death and love that were pushing me through the night sky, toward France. I let the warm tears fall, grateful that in the darkness, no one could see. The huge jet engines droned and finally, I slept.

The next morning in Paris, I took the R.E.R. train into the city and then the Metro to the Gare Saint-Lazare, to catch the train to Normandy. As soon as I bought my ticket, I called Huguette to tell her when I was arriving. I napped during the two-hour journey, my head against the cold glass of the rattling train window, as it passed through the colorless winter landscape.

When I stepped off the train in Caen, I started searching the faces of the crowd, looking for Gilbert. Then I remembered. Gilbert wouldn't be coming this time, or ever again, to meet me at the train. It felt so sad, so final.

I spotted Cathy, their daughter, in the crowd. We exchanged the special four kisses, then looked at each other and both started to cry. People don't hug in France the way we do in America, but we hugged each other, standing there in the train station in Caen on that cold winter evening, with people rushing past all around us.

At their house, Huguette greeted me warmly. She'd fixed me a delicious soup and after a bowl, I went straight up to what felt like "my room," the guest room, to sleep. I'd been traveling almost twenty-four hours, but I had made it. I had arrived in time for the funeral.

The next morning, the family gathered at the mortuary to sit with Gilbert's body for the last time. He looked frail and thin, lying in the casket, not like his usual robust and exuberant self, but I said goodbye to the physical form that had carried his heart and soul.

I remembered how I had sat with the bodies of my father, my sister and then my mother, such a powerful wake-up call to the preciousness of life. I wished I'd been able to come back to visit sooner. But it felt intimate and deep to be in the inner circle of the family as we sat with Gilbert's body and grieved his loss.

The word "family" could be defined as the people with whom you share your joys and your sorrows. Sometimes you're related to them by blood and sometimes you're not. That day, as I sat with them in the small room at the mortuary, saying goodbye to Gilbert, I knew I was their family and they were mine.

In Gilbert's tiny village, bells tolled as relatives and friends braved the chilly, gray day to gather at the church for his funeral. We waited outside as an honor guard of fellow Veterans carried his coffin, draped by the tricolor French flag, into the church.

My breath came out in clouds and I shivered down into my thick wool coat. As I reached up to pull my scarf tighter, I happened to feel the pulse in my neck, steady and strong, thump, thump, thump, such a reminder that I was alive and well on that freezing morning that I was saying goodbye to my French brother.

I sat in the front pew between Huguette and Cathy. During the service, the priest asked me to place a photo of my father and one of Gilbert from 1944, together in one frame, on the coffin. There was a slight murmur as I did that—everyone in the packed church knew the story. I felt honored to be a part of the service and to have Dad remembered at that moment too.

They played a Celine Dion song, "*S'il suffisait d'aimer,*" "If it is enough to Love." I remembered playing that song for Gilbert and Huguette when they visited me in Aix-en-Provence. As I let in the music and the words, I thought, *Yes, it is enough to love. It is more than enough. It is everything.*

The priest spoke about Gilbert's life and as I listened to the words honoring him, I realized again that if Gilbert had become my American brother, the French story would have ended there. Instead, over six decades later, I sat as part of Gilbert's family, in his village in France.

Candlelight flickered on the faces of the handsome young Naval officer and the sweet little boy as we prayed, sang and sat in silence.

Cathy had been right. It was *le destin* that my father and Gilbert had loved each other and then had to say goodbye. As the music echoed off the walls of the old church, I knew it had also been my destiny, linked by their love across space and time, to bring them back together, and to fulfill my father's promise.

After the church service, the family returned to the funeral home. We sat in a small room with Gilbert's coffin, the man in charge said a few words, then the coffin moved away on a track, through some doors, toward being cremated. The cultural anthropologist in me found this difference from America interesting, though a little startling. It seemed to draw out the process of saying goodbye and Huguette was weeping. Yet there was also a finality. When those doors closed, he was gone forever.

Close friends and family gathered back at the house for a luncheon. Extra leaves expanded the dining table and everyone crowded around. I was so grateful for my ability to understand the chatter of the conversation and to participate. I even told the story about how Dad's French teacher made "*s'il vous plaît*" sound like "silver plate." They all laughed. I'd never told a story in French before and gotten a laugh.

Huguette struggled with the emptiness and grief of losing Gilbert, her husband of almost fifty years. My presence seemed to comfort her and it gave her daughter Cathy a little breather, so I stayed five more days. We visited the cemetery each day, and went to a special mass for Gilbert. At home, we ate her delicious food and rested.

The day that I left, Huguette and her grandson Romain drove me to the train station in Caen. Romain had been a boy of twelve when they visited California; now he was twenty-three. We shivered together in the February cold as we waited on the platform.

When the train screeched to a halt, Romain hefted my bag up for me and Huguette waved and blew kisses as the train pulled away. I waved until I couldn't see them anymore, wiping away tears and trying to compose myself as the train rattled down the tracks and headed back to Paris.

I left knowing that losing someone you care about is the same in any language. And with Gilbert and my father both gone, that chapter of the story was over. But the light of the love that they shared lived on, in me, in Huguette and in everyone who knew the story.

I arrived back in Paris and took the #21 bus across town to my hotel in the Latin Quarter and spent the chilly, rainy day walking the streets of Paris. At Notre Dame Cathedral, I prayed and lit a candle for Gilbert and all the loved ones I'd lost. The quiet and reverence of the ancient cathedral soothed and calmed me. The sun came out around sunset, lighting up the bridges crossing the Seine as I hurried back to my hotel.

A few days later, I began my planned itinerary, which included seawater spa treatments in La Baule, a truffle hunt in the Dordogne and then on to my beloved Aix-en-Provence. Near the end of the trip, I arrived in Aix late at night at the old train station and for a moment, couldn't remember which way to walk to get to the *centre- ville*, the center of town.

Someone pointed out the way and after five minutes, I felt the relief of seeing the main street, *Cours Mirabeau* with its giant fountain. I checked into my hotel, feeling safe and secure in my "home town" in France once again.

The next few days, as I walked around Aix, reconnecting with Maïté and other old friends, it felt like I'd never left, though I'd been gone almost eight years. As I was buying some apples at the open market, talking to the farmer and exchanging pleasantries, I felt a moment of pure happiness and contentment.

How mysterious happiness is. It comes in little spurts that always feel like a gift, even a surprise. They're unpredictable and erratic, but so welcome. After the sadness of losing Gilbert, the moment felt like a balm.

I saw how being in France and speaking French, the language of my soul, made me happy, another mystery. I decided at that moment that I was not going to question any more the why or wherefore of happiness. I was going to enjoy it and count the blessings of it, wherever they came from.

Epilogue

As I write this, ten years have passed since being with my French family at Gilbert's funeral. The years have brought so many blessings. I married a wonderful man and we travel most summers to Europe. On several trips, we have stayed at Lake Annecy and I was able to fulfill the vow from my first visit to France, to visit that beautiful area again. But best of all, I have been able to keep in close contact with Huguette and the family with almost yearly visits.

In 2014, I traveled to France for the 70th anniversary of D-Day with Stephen Ambrose Historical Tours again as a guide and translator between the Veterans and the French. After the tour, Huguette and I were able to enjoy a long visit.

Romain, their grandson, married a lovely woman, Vanessa and they have two beautiful children, a girl and a boy. Their son Tim, age eight, knows how to say, "hello, goodbye and 'my name is Tim, what is yours?" Very cute.

Grandson Benoît finished his education and secured a very good job that required him to learn English. On my recent visit last summer, we spoke a few words together, the first English I have ever spoken with Gilbert's family.

I continue to work on my French between visits so that I can keep up with the family conversations, which move very fast. When I'm there, the same worn French/English dictionary sits handy by the dining-room table, when needed. Benoît and his partner, Marion, are planning a visit to

California and I look forward to hosting them at my farm. He will be able to practice his English and I'm sure we'll still speak French.

It has been a pleasure to continue and deepen my relationship with Huguette. Somehow, I feel that Gilbert, my father and my sister Sharon all know that I have a true French sister in Huguette.

On our last visit, I was showing her, as always, the recent photos of the family, of my daughters and of all the grandchildren who have come along since their visit to California twenty-one years ago. At one point, she started to cry and I reached out and put my hand over hers. The two of us were feeling the power and poignancy of our relationship as we sat together at the table. Our love and friendship has stood the test of time.

Twenty-five years ago, in 1993, when I traveled to France to research the essay for the upcoming 50th anniversary of D-Day, I had no idea the stream of events that would be set in motion by that story. It's easy to see, looking back, the fragility of all the connections on my return trip in 1994 and to feel the wonder and gratitude of how it came together. This was all before cellphones and email—any "misses" would have been fatal.

That newspaper story, not only led me to Gilbert and fourteen years of having him as a brother, but now, twenty-four years later, gives me an ongoing relationship with his family, my French family, that spans four generations.

The late John O'Donohue talked about how we're being "minded" in our lives, guided by unseen hands. Looking back over almost seven decades of life, I can feel the mystery of all the times and places where that has been true in my life. I can also see how our dreams and passions open a doorway to our destinies.

For all of the years that I was pulled back to studying French, I had no way to explain the wonder the language held for me and still holds for me. The joy I feel when I speak it, the pleasurable sensation of my brain remembering which sounds to make when, the miracle of being understood. From the first moment I heard *chambre meublée* when I was twelve years old, I could feel another life calling out to me and pulling me towards it. And that life led me to Gilbert.

My father was a storyteller. He passed that down to me. Maybe that is why I've been compelled to be a writer, to be the "keeper of the stories" in my family and in my life.

In one year, we will celebrate the 75th anniversary of D-Day, three quarters of a century since this story began with my father and Gilbert on the cliff above Omaha Beach.

I hope that this story will remind others of the power of love and kindness and even of the power of stories to soothe and calm us.

We're here to love and be loved. Everything else is like cotton candy—it looks pretty, but then you discover that there is no real substance to it, no real nourishment there.

Someone said, "In the end, it's all about who you love and letting them know." That is true. I know that now.

I look forward to the continued unfolding and legacy of this story, through the years and across time and space.

I wish you blessings on your lives and on your stories of love.

May they bring you, and those around you, great joy.

Diane Covington-Carter
Nevada City, California,
June 2018

Acknowledgements

To all the members of my writing circle, who listened as this work distilled itself into words on the page, week after week, month after month.

To my Writing Angels, Marilee Ford, Susan Prilliman, Heather Williams, Cheryl Murray, Vincent D'Ath and Landon Carter, who read my final draft to help me to know if I was done.

To Sands Hall, writer and editor extraordinaire, who helped me to polish the story for *Reader's Digest*, which then propelled me to write the book. Also Diane Goullard, who provided professional editing and looked for French errors.

To the press attaché at the French Consulate, Chantal Haag, who encouraged me to place the ad to find Gilbert.

To my dear friend, Maïté le Dantec, who also checked my French to make sure it was correct.

To Tom Milam, for getting me to France in 1993 so that I could write that first essay.

To Margaret Jean Campbell for patient and tireless help with cover design and layout and Margie Baxley, a wizard at all things technical.

To all the readers of the essay published in the *Reader's Digest* who tracked me down to tell me how much the story meant to them.

To Stephen Ambrose Historical Tours, for hiring me as a guide and translator for the 60th and 70th anniversaries of D-Day, giving me such rich chances to immerse myself in the history and reality of the Normandy Invasion.

To my daughters, Michelle and Heather, for being on the journey of life with me.

And finally, to my husband, Landon Carter, for his unfailing patience, love and support as I struggled in the deep and powerful work necessary to complete this book. The space he held for me made all the difference.

Author's note

In addition to my father's stories, I have read countless books on the Normandy Invasion and World War II and have learned a lot by participating in three D-Day anniversary celebrations in France, the 50th, 60th and 70th.

I owe thanks to the many Veterans who have told their stories on websites, describing in detail the scene on Omaha Beach, when they landed on D-Day, the bodies, the sea red with the blood of the dead young men, their own horror, pain and struggles to survive. Also, movies such as *Saving Private Ryan* and *The Longest Day* have portrayed the invasion in realistic detail.

In 2004, Captain Bill Hilderbrand, Civil Engineer Corps, U.S. Navy (Retired), President of the C.E.C./Seabee Historical Foundation, gave me a list of survivors from Dad's 111th Seabee battalion, which allowed me the chance to talk to both officers and enlisted men.

One of the sailors, William (Bill) Rostich, remembered Dad and his relationship with Gilbert, and provided me with valuable information that allowed me to piece together more details for some of the scenes for this book.

Rostich told me about the baseball games in the evening and also remembered that Dad made Gilbert take a shower, during which Gilbert howled. Knowing my father, I guessed that there was a reason for that shower, besides Dad loving for his children to be clean.

It would have been so much like my father to buy Gilbert some new clothes to have after Dad left, to remember him by, as Dad did for me before we parted when I was eighteen.

At the Seabee museum in Port Hueneme, California, I had access to all the records from Dad's battalion from 1943-1945. I read papers documenting how Dad and his team went back and forth to Bayeux for a week for a restoration project and knew that the village had not been destroyed during the invasion, meaning Dad would have had access to shops during that time. I was not able to verify this fact with Gilbert however before he died, so need to be forgiven for possible artistic license in that scene about the clothes.

My research at the Seabee museum was also so helpful in providing facts about Dad's experience in Normandy. For example, I read the hand-written list of assignments for D-Day, with my father's team going in on D-Day plus 1 and saw when Dad's duties included being "the officer of the day."

That research and those boxes of papers gave me a more complete picture of life in France during my father's time there, but also details that helped to fill out the story. I saw the exact date that Dad left Normandy in late October, for example, telling me how long Dad and Gilbert were together, almost five months. I saw photos of the evening baseball and football games and other rare photos of Dad and his men.

Dad's military records, which I was able to obtain as a family member, also helped to fill in details. That's where I learned that he was one of the officers in charge of building the Rhino Ferries. Dad was not one to draw attention to himself or to brag. He also never mentioned the fact that he had won a medal for sharpshooting during his training or been a champion boxer in college, details which came from his military records.

I also learned a lot from reading my parents' letters from that time. My father pleaded with my mother to write more. She was busy going to dances, which created tension with my father's parents, with whom she was staying on their farm. They would have been babysitting my two older brothers, Clark and Kenton, one and three when my mother went out dancing.

In writing a story like this, the facts create the structure, which needs to be filled out with details that can't always be verified. I so wish I had asked a million more questions before my father and Gilbert died. So, for example, I'm not sure of the exact menu that the Navy camp served at lunch and dinner. I had to guess based on the typical American diet, meat and potatoes, during that time period.

I did learn that the Navy camp had a reputation for the best food and the best hot showers—leave it to the Seabees to figure out how to create the hot showers.

It is comforting to think that the millions of soldiers who passed through the camp on their way east to fight at least had a good meal and a hot shower before their ordeals ahead.

About the author

Diane Covington-Carter graduated with honors from UCLA and has received awards for her writing, photography and NPR commentaries. She lives in Northern California and New Zealand with her husband and travels to France as often as possible. Her other books are: *Eight Months in Provence, A Junior Year Abroad, Thirty Years Late, (2016)*

And *Falling in Love Backwards, an Unlikely Tale of Happily Ever After (2013),* co-authored with her husband, Landon Carter.

Visit her website at www.dianecovingtoncarter.com

Made in the USA
San Bernardino, CA
14 June 2019